THE NORTHWEST COOKBOOK

THE NORTHWEST

LIVING WITH ABUNDANCE IN THE PACIFIC

COOKBOOK
NORTHWEST

By
Lila Gault

Illustrations by Peggy Sheehan

New York · London · Tokyo

International Standard Book Number: 0-8256-3089-4
Library of Congress Catalog Card Number: 78-056216

Printed in the United States of America.

Book design by Ede Dreikurs
Illustrations by Peggy Sheehan
Cover photograph by Herbert Wise

To Elizabeth Underwood and all of our grandmothers, for whom living with abundance was not a matter of choice.

More than two dozen friends contributed to this book. Some gave recipes, others tales of gathering abundance, and the rest a lot of invaluable support. Libby Anderson, a restaurateur and true professional, shared selflessly of her time, talents, and unending volume of recipes. John Strait and Jim Doerty were also especially willing to share their culinary expertise. Gale Cool and Jerry Mahony contributed great hunting stories and many recipes. And special thanks to my husband, Mac Kennedy, for his patience, enthusiasm, and culinary inspiration. In our kitchen, he is the master chef.

CONTENTS

INTRODUCTION
1

A NOTE ABOUT EQUIPMENT
5

A NOTE ABOUT HERBS
6

SPRING
9

ASPARAGUS
10

CHICKEN AND EGGS
13

PLANTING THE VEGETABLE GARDEN
25

SPRINGTIME PICNICKING
34

SUMMER
41

PIKE PLACE MARKET
42

SUMMERTIME FRUIT
43

WILD AND DOMESTIC BERRIES
49

CLAMS AND MORE CLAMS
59

SALMON
67

BOTTOM FISH
79

CHEESE AND COMPANY
87

GARDEN VEGETABLES
90

FALL
107

GRAPES AND WINE
107

APPLES AND SWEET CIDER
109

APPLE WINE AND SPARKLING CIDER
114

APPLES FOR EATING
118

MUSHROOM HUNTING
127

HUNTING FOR DEER AND ELK
141

HUNTING FOR GAME BIRDS
145

LATE GARDEN VEGETABLES
154

PEARS
162

FILBERTS
165

PRESERVING THE HARVEST
167

WINTER

WINTER   173
DUNGENESS CRAB   174
PRAWNS AND SHRIMP   178
OYSTERS   183
MUSSELS   188
SQUID AND OCTOPUS   190
ABALONE AND SCALLOPS   192
STEELHEAD TROUT   192
SOURDOUGH   195
SCANDINAVIAN CHRISTMAS SPECIALTIES   199
HOLIDAY FAVORITES   201
CHRISTMAS DINNER   207

INDEX   212

INTRODUCTION

Although the moon was nearly full, it was not quite bright enough to light our way to the beach. But with the help of several kerosene lanterns, the search began shortly before midnight. Three of us worked quickly with shovels and pitchforks, filling buckets with dozens of steamer clams, a few of their larger cousins, and as many rock crab as could be spotted on the shallow bottom. The unusually low tide revealed a long, flat rock, thickly covered with mussels that could be pried away from the surface with ease. Returning to the kitchen with the bounty, we planned a fishing excursion for daybreak in hopes of catching a rock cod or two.

Why all this midnight activity? There was something to celebrate, and a dozen friends had been invited for a dinner of Puget Sound bouillabaisse. Early the next morning, the clams, crab and mussels were cleaned and made ready for the pot, along with two large freshly caught fish. After the seafood was all prepared, a savory stock was brought to life and put on the back burner on top of the stove to simmer for the rest of the afternoon.

When the guests arrived that evening, all of the natural abundance was tossed into the stew, and almost immediately dinner was ready. The preparation was not difficult and the results were elegant. Accompanied by several loaves of homemade sourdough bread, a tartly dressed green salad, and a jug of vin ordinaire, *this delightful seafood stew was but one of many memorable culinary adventures of that particular season.*

There is perhaps more gathering and preparation of naturally abundant foods in the Pacific Northwest than in almost any other region in the United States. During the last hundred years, many of these foods have also been successfully cultivated. One of the most fertile growing zones in the nation, the Northwest produces fruit, vegetables, and wheat that are shipped in great quantities throughout the world. Such prosperity is not the sole monopoly of agribusiness, however, as thousands of backyard gardeners in the Pacific Northwest will attest. Almost anyone with a small plot of ground and a handful of seeds can successfully grow much of what they eat.

Inspired by the specialties of each season and encouraged by a nearly inexhaustible supply of local abundance, Northwest cuisine is truly more of an attitude toward food than a particular method defined by arbitrary rules. The result is a simple, but careful style of cooking that largely depends on the skill and imagination of the cook. A natural rhythm based on seasonal specialties flows through most Northwest kitchens. These specialties provide a source of continual inspiration for dedicated Northwest cooks.

I have included here a variety of recipes featuring the native plenty of Washington, Oregon, and British Columbia—especially that from the coastal regions bounded by the Pacific Ocean on the west and the Cascade Mountains to the east. Most of this fare is found in the woods, lakes, forests, and ocean, and can be brought into the kitchen just a few hours before the guests arrive for dinner. Many others of these ingredients can be purchased at local markets and roadside stands.

For those without immediate access to fresh salmon, wild mushrooms, or live geoduck, I suggest that this book be used for inspiration as well as advice. Consider the recipes as guides rather than formulas, and substitute your own local abundance for ours.

Any regional cuisine reflects its ethnic history as well as local abundance. The Northwest has been blessed with the arrival of many different cultural communities who now call this bountiful region home. Both Japanese and Chinese immigrants have long-established enclaves in Seattle and Vancouver. Swedes, Norwegians, and Finns settled throughout the Northwest in large numbers and have maintained many of their Scandinavian traditions. Equally important are the original settlers—the Indians of the mountain and coastal regions—to whom credit should be properly given for what most Americans consider the quintessential Northwest feast—the salmon barbecue.

Freshness of fare, simplicity in preparation, and touches of ethnic influence are the cornerstones of Pacific Northwest cuisine. But barely a century old, the style is still evolving. It is being perfected in restaurants by those professionals whose business is fine food. It continues to develop and grow in kitchens throughout Puget Sound, along the Columbia River, and beside the Georgia Strait. It's a cuisine for every season and one for those who cook, as well as for those who simply enjoy food.

Spring, 1978

A NOTE ABOUT EQUIPMENT

Most culinary experts feel that if Escoffier were alive today, he would use a Cuisinart or one of the less expensive food processors. A few of those who teach and write about food continue to extol the virtues of a strong, sharp knife and put the food processor down as a passing fad. I concur with the traditionalists; a basic set of skillets, saucepans, and a Dutch oven or two will allow you to prepare almost any recipe in this book. A few require easily obtainable special equipment.

Cast-iron utensils may be heavy and often cumbersome, but they are universally recognized as the best for most stove-top cooking because they conduct and retain heat evenly and efficiently. They must be treated with care, though, as cast iron will rust, stain, and even absorb certain flavors. I wipe out my skillets with a paper towel or a damp sponge and avoid cleaning them with soap and water. When a pan gets ruined—which can happen when a "hot spot" occurs—it is easy to replace from a local hardware store.

It is tempting to acquire a great deal of paraphernalia in the course of setting up the ideal kitchen. And although I am all for ginger graters, lemon zesters, and chinois for those who have the space and budget to accommodate them, there is really only one special tool that I find absolutely essential—a good strong garlic press. Mashed or pressed garlic is basic to many of the recipes in this book; and the best way to mash garlic is with a good press. The inexpensive models should be avoided in favor of the imported heavy aluminum type, which works better and will last for years.

Cast-iron cookware, a few carbon-steel knives, and an aluminum garlic press are a good beginning, but these don't quite furnish the entire kitchen, even for a back-to-basics equipment buyer like me. Every cook will develop equipment preferences and favorites. These are mine, almost all of which I use at least once a week. For the sake of brevity, I have shortened the designations of some of this equipment in the recipes throughout the book—these designations are indicated by the quoted terms in the following lists.

Pots, Pans, and Skillets

8-inch cast-iron frying pan—"medium frying pan"
12-inch cast-iron frying pan—"large frying pan"
10-inch aluminum omelet pan
1-quart cast-iron saucepan—"small saucepan"
1½-quart cast-iron saucepan—"medium saucepan"
2½-quart cast-iron saucepan—"large saucepan"
Stainless steel or aluminum wok

5-quart casserole—"Dutch oven"
8-quart casserole—"large Dutch oven" or "stockpot"
1-quart glass double boiler
(All of these pieces should have tight-fitting lids)

Baking Dishes

8-by-8 inch shallow baking dish, aluminum or glass—"square baking pan"
9-by-16 inch shallow baking dish, cast iron—"long baking pan"
4 bread pans, aluminum, glass, or baker's steel
2 baking sheets, baker's steel
Muffin tin, aluminum or baker's steel
9-inch pie pan, glass
10-inch pie pan, glass

Special Equipment

Copper bowl
Balloon whisk
Soufflé dish
Ceramic bread bowl
Vegetable steamer
Garlic press
Fish poacher
Wooden spoons
Rubber spatulas
Carbon-steel knives—paring, boning, slicing, cleaver
Blender

A NOTE ABOUT HERBS

The creative use of herbs and spices can turn an ordinary supper into an elegant feast. For those of us who routinely prepare fresh fruit, vegetables, fish, and game, home-grown herbs seem to taste just a little bit better than commercial ones, even those from specialty spice shops. Whether they are used fresh or dried, herbs from a window box or backyard corner are essential to the best preparation of all sorts of seasonal abundance.

Although herbs are generally picked and used fresh in the summer, during the rest of the year they are usually available in dried form. Different methods of drying herbs should be used, depending on the part of the plant that the grower plans to save. Leaves should be picked individually, placed on trays covered with cheesecloth, and left in a well-ventilated, dimly lit room for several days until they are completely dry. Seeds are usually left on the stalk, which is pulled from the ground and then hung upside down. The seeds can be removed when they are partially dry and put on trays for complete drying.

Garlic and shallots are never dried for use. They are harvested, braided into strings using their long slender leaves, and hung in the kitchen. Horseradish should be freshly ground just before using.

All dried herbs need to be stored in airtight containers to ensure maximum longevity and strength. Since dried herbs are about three times as potent as fresh ones, they should be used especially carefully. I grow the following herbs in a small garden just outside my kitchen door. They will all grow well in a moderate climate such as the Pacific Northwest.

―――――――――――― **Basil in several varieties** ――――――――――――
Caraway
Chives
Coriander
Dill
Fennel
Garlic
Horseradish
Marjoram
Mint in several varieties
Oregano
Parsley
Rosemary
Sage
Savory, summer and winter varieties
Shallots
Tarragon
Thyme
Watercress
――――――――――――― **Woodruff** ―――――――――――――

SPRING

Spring comes on tiptoe in the Pacific Northwest, west of the Cascade Mountains following winters that are usually mild and relatively warm. There is no "in like a lion and out like a lamb" for March or for any other spring month here. Instead we have a gradual warming that begins as early as February and sometimes as late as May. The skies remain gray and inscrutable regardless of change in the surface temperature, and the rain continues for most of the spring season. Spring often segues into summer before many of us realize that winter is even over.

The dedicated seasonal observer eagerly anticipates the traditional indicators of spring. Here, as in most other parts of the country, the crocus is usually the first sure sign. Its slender leaves shoot out of the ground almost overnight and are shortly followed by a delicate white, yellow, or purple blossom. The crocus will often appear as early as Washington's Birthday in Puget Sound. And if the croci are up and the weather is warm, the end of February finds many a local gardener out planting the garden peas. More often than not, however, March rains rot these peas before they can germinate. But in those few years when the crop takes hold, the early planting really pays off. Peas can be harvested by the first of May—the first reward after finishing the task of planting the entire garden.

As in other coastal regions, the northward bird migration brings great ex-

citement to the Pacific Northwest in the spring. The geese come first, both Canada and snow, followed by numerous species of ducks, terns, and other water birds. Then come the backyard favorites, such as the Alaska robin, Steller's jay, and a myriad of warblers. Finally the barn swallows, chimney swifts, and hummingbirds appear and begin to build their homes for the season in convenient orchards and outbuildings.

On the other side of the Cascades in both Washington and Oregon, the arrival of spring is an unmistakable event. Winters are long and bitterly cold at times, so the warmer days are greeted with great relief. New life comes to the frozen lakes and rivers when the spring thaw begins in earnest. As the blanket of snow recedes and disappears, everything turns beautifully green for a few weeks. Spring is the only season of natural green in this region, because the summer green is the result of massive irrigation.

Asparagus

The pursuit and preparation of wild foods is the pastime of many people in the Pacific Northwest. Yet seldom are the rewards as great as in the spring when the wild asparagus is at its peak. Since it is exactly the same species as the domestic variety, eager hunters sally forth in great numbers. Asparagus is not only a treat to the palate, but also to the eye. Once the choice spears have been harvested, the remaining ones send up beautiful lacy green foliage. This greenery lines creekbeds and irrigation canals throughout central Washington long into the summer.

Several friends and I gather wild asparagus at least once during the season. We usually head southeast from Seattle over Chinook Pass, itself somewhat southeast of Mount Rainier. The drive is always a pleasure, as we pass through several small towns and on to the untouched forests of Mount Rainier National Park. Chinook Pass is always closed by several dozen feet of snow in the winter and has usually just reopened by the time we make the asparagus trek.

Exceptional views of Mount Rainier can be had from the road, as it winds through what appear to be foothills, but which are really four- and five-thousand-foot peaks themselves. Even on a cloudy day when the mountain is completely enveloped in fog, one can feel its extraordinary presence. But on a clear day, the mountain dominates the surrounding countryside without the slightest inclination to share centerstage.

Making this trip one year, we finally passed Rainier and headed down the eastern slope of the Cascade range. On this side of the mountains the forest is mostly pine growing in dry and rocky soil. The thick carpet of underbrush commonly found in the Douglas fir, cedar, and hemlock forests of the Puget Sound area is strikingly absent.

Not far from the city of Yakima, center of the remarkably fertile Yakima Valley, we spotted the first stand of asparagus. Quickly pulling off the road and gathering small knives and big sacks, we approached a long irrigation ditch, partially filled with water. A dozen or so little green spears nestled under old growth from the previous season. Bright green and as long as an outstretched hand from fingertip to palm, the spears broke readily at the base.

Our party of three easily gathered fifty pounds that day. All that was required for successful hunting was a gathering bag, nimble fingers, and enthusiasm. One day's haul meant plenty of fresh asparagus for several weeks, and some left over for freezing.

Some of my favorite ways to prepare this delicious spring treat include cream of asparagus soup, asparagus soufflé, or chilled asparagus with a tart vinaigrette dressing. Asparagus is also superb when it is baked, sauced, and sprinkled with a variety of cheeses, especially freshly grated Parmesan.

It is simple to freeze fresh asparagus and it maintains its firm texture better than most frozen vegetables. Simply trim the spears into 6-inch lengths, or smaller pieces if desired, immerse them briefly in boiling water, drain well, and wrap in plastic bags for freezer storage.

–Cream of Asparagus—
Soup

1 cup water
1 lb. fresh asparagus,
   chopped into 1-inch pieces
1 small white onion, finely chopped
3 tablespoons butter
2½ cups chicken stock
3 tablespoons flour
2 teaspoons dill weed
2 tablespoons lemon juice
2 cups light cream
Salt and pepper
Sour cream for garnish

Place water in large saucepan and bring to a boil. Reduce heat, add asparagus, and steam for 6 minutes or until very tender. Melt butter in medium frying pan and sauté onions until tender.

Purée both vegetables in blender and return to saucepan. Add stock, flour, dill, and lemon juice. Stir over low heat until thickened. Remove from heat and add cream, salt and pepper to taste, and blend thoroughly.

Serve chilled with a dollop of sour cream. Serves 6.

–Asparagus Vinaigrette

1 lb. fresh asparagus, trimmed
  and cut into 4-inch pieces
½ cup olive oil
3 tablespoons white wine vinegar
1 small garlic clove, mashed
1 tablespoon fresh chives,
  finely chopped
¼ teaspoon salt
Freshly ground black pepper to taste
4 large lettuce leaves,
  washed and patted dry
Capers

In Dutch oven, steam asparagus until tender, but firm. Combine oil, vinegar, garlic, chives, salt, and pepper in small jar with tight lid and shake well. Place several spears of asparagus on each lettuce leaf and pour dressing over top. Garnish with capers and chill before serving. Serves 4.

–Baked Asparagus

3 tablespoons butter
3 tablespoons flour
2½ cups milk
Salt and pepper to taste
2 lbs. fresh asparagus,
  trimmed of woody ends
2 cups Cheddar cheese, grated
½ cup chopped almonds

In large saucepan, melt butter, add flour, and cook over low heat for 2 minutes, stirring constantly. Add milk and simmer, stirring constantly, for ten minutes or until thickened. Add salt and pepper and stir. Place asparagus in bottom of greased long baking pan, cover with half of sauce, then sprinkle cheese and almonds over top. Cover with remaining sauce and bake at 350° for 20 minutes. Serves 6.

CHICKEN AND EGGS

Although I would hardly boast that the Pacific Northwest has any regional monopoly on the species, the western Washington chicken merits a certain national distinction—thanks to Betty MacDonald's eloquence in The Egg and I. *Perhaps inspired by MacDonald's example, a number of otherwise non-farmers in the Pacific Northwest have become the keepers of a back-yard flock. I am one of those who only needed to find out that chickens are virtually self-maintaining before I got my own rooster and hens.*

Chickens need to be well penned where I live. There are too many raccoons, weasels, and neighborhood dogs who can and will make life extremely hazardous for chickens. All kinds of existing structures are converted to chicken houses—from falling-down garages to abandoned outhouses. Some ambitious chicken keepers prefer to build new coops and, in the process, let their architectural imaginations run wild.

My chickens live in what I fondly refer to as "the palace," a henhouse built more than forty years ago by someone who must have raised a good-sized flock. There are six nesting boxes, an area for enclosing the mother hen and her chicks, and two long roosting poles. More than a dozen chickens can live very comfortably there, but my flock rarely numbers more than ten.

My "ladies" eat as many green trimmings and discards as I can provide, in addition to a basic diet of chicken meal. They particularly seem to like carrot tops and lettuce that has gone to seed, but blackberry vines will also nicely augment their daily supply of grubs, meal, and other greens. In return for this small amount of attention, seven hens give me over three dozen eggs every week. This is almost one egg per hen every day. There is always one hen at the bottom of the pecking order who rarely lays. She is just too busy being harassed by her sisters to even think about producing her share.

Winter is the quiet season for chickens. If there are even two eggs in the nesting boxes every day, I consider myself quite lucky. As the weather starts to warm in March, one or two of the hens gets "broody." Soon she is sitting on twelve to fifteen eggs with unusual determination.

The other hens usually ignore their sitting sister, but the rooster gives her extra protection. Caruso, as my favorite rooster is affectionately known, demonstrates the operatic prowess of his namesake with both lusty voice and proud strutting around the coop anytime, but especially when a hen gets broody. He seems to know that he is partly responsible for the hen's condition.

About two and a half to three weeks after the hen has begun to set, signs of life begin to appear in the nest. Several of the eggs start talking and the mother becomes very anxious. It is impossible to move her off the nest at this stage, so one must be patient and content to listen to the activity underneath the hen's outspread wings. The hen responds to the noises from the shells and soon one chick will begin to peck its way out of the shell. It emerges very wet and scrawny in appearance, but the hen's body heat soon dries out the new feathers and the bird begins to look more round. After one pops out, the others soon follow, and within forty-eight hours all of the chicks have left their shells.

The mother hen continues to sit on her flock until every chick is hatched. By this time the first ones are hungry and ready to eat. The mother finds grubs for her chicks to supplement the special meal and water provided by the caretaker. Chicks and mother all like to stay in the coop for ten to twelve days. The chicks peep frequently and often climb under their mother to stay warm.

The hen shepherds her chicks until they are two months old. By then they are quite large and ready to fend for themselves. The hen has usually grown tired of mothering this particular group, but is often ready to start another batch.

A hen starts to lay when she is four to five months old and usually continues through three laying seasons. She quits every year for a brief molting period, but that eggless time can be shortened by supplying additional greens. This dietary boost encourages the new growth of feathers.

I am so spoiled by immediate access to fresh eggs that I probably use many more eggs in cooking than most people. Weekend breakfasts nearly always include fried eggs one morning and French toast or waffles the next. I generally have an omelet or soufflé for dinner once a week and bake a tremendous amount of cakes and quick breads with the rest of my weekly supply.

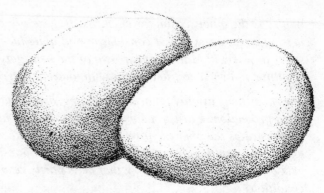

Soufflés

Sweet and savory soufflés both rate very high on my list of elegant and worthwhile culinary endeavors. I have found that every soufflé will be a guaranteed success with the help of a few special tools, an oven that maintains an even temperature, and the use of impeccably fresh ingredients, including fresh eggs.

I know of no satisfactory substitute for the soufflé dish. Not only essential for the soufflé itself, this handsome porcelain baking dish, which can also be made of glass or stoneware, doubles nicely as a salad bowl. I use a soufflé dish imported from France, which after years of wear still maintains an even glaze and even lip.

Soufflés also require a copper bowl and a balloon whisk for beating the egg whites. A chemical reaction between the metal and the eggs allows the cook to whip properly stiffened egg whites in minutes. My copper bowl is an inexpensive spun-metal type. There are others, of course, which cost more.

If you do not have a copper bowl, you can certainly still make a soufflé. A bit of cream of tartar can be added to the egg whites to ensure quick and proper stiffening when beaten.

Always let the eggs reach room temperature before separating for use in a soufflé. Chilled eggs are more difficult to separate and do not beat as easily.

–Savory Soufflé

This basic savory soufflé can be made with almost any pureed vegetable or grated cheese. I often experiment with what ever vegetable from my garden is ready for harvest and have had great success with broccoli, asparagus, and parsnips. Different herbs and seasonings may be tried as well; some of my favorites include caraway, dill, and chives.

The unorthodox wheat-germ crust on my soufflés gives the results an in-teresting texture.

> **3 tablespoons butter**
> **3 tablespoons flour**
> **¾ cup milk**
> **½ cup light cream**
> **½ teaspoon salt**
> **¼ teaspoon white pepper**
> **6 medium eggs, separated**
> **1 cup puréed vegetables**
>   ***and/or* ½ cup grated cheese**
> **1 tablespoon butter**
> **¼ cup raw wheat germ**

In medium frying pan melt butter, add flour, and cook over low heat for 3 minutes, stirring constantly. Slowly add milk, cream, salt, and pepper. Stir until completely smooth and slightly thickened. Remove from heat and add egg yolks. Return to low heat for scant minute, stirring carefully. Add puréed vegetables and additional seasonings, stir well, and remove from heat.

Grease 1½ quart dish with 1 tablespoon butter and coat bottom and sides with wheat germ. Beat egg whites in copper bowl until stiff. Carefully blend half of egg whites into vegetable mixture. Pour into soufflé dish and blend in rest of whites, being careful not to lift wheat germ from sides of dish, until color is even. Bake at 375° for 30 minutes, or 5 minutes more for firmer soufflé. Serves 2–3.

–Sweet Soufflés ——————

A sweet soufflé is a very special treat, destined to be featured at Sunday brunch or as a elegant dessert. It can even be a memorable alternative to the traditional birthday cake.

Various fruits in season work well as additions to the basic recipe. I like puréed fresh peaches or plums in the summer or a berry sauce from the freezer in the winter. To make a sweet soufflé, substitute 1 cup of fruit for the vegetable in the savory soufflé recipe above, and always add 2 ta-blespoons of confectioner's sugar to sweeten the egg-and-milk mixture, and omit the salt and pepper.

Liqueur is a classic addition to the sweet soufflé. Almost any liqueur can be successfully substituted for the cream listed in the basic recipe. Confec-

tioner's sugar is especially important when alcohol is used.

Different combinations of fruits and liqueurs can be memorable. I like cognac and plums, peaches and Grand Marnier, and Mandarin oranges and Israeli Sabra. When the soufflé comes out of the oven, it can be dusted lightly with confectioner's sugar and should then be served at once. Bon appetit!

Omelets

As for a soufflé, the secret to a successful omelet is good equipment and fresh ingredients. The well-seasoned omelet pan is a kitchen essential and should be exclusively restricted to use for omelets. My pan is aluminum with a rough sandcast finish and a wooden handle. This particular pan has held its initial seasoning faultlessly and conducts heat evenly and quickly. In addition, it is very easy to manipulate, which is a major consideration for a functional omelet pan.

The classic omelet is one of the creative cook's most challenging opportunities. Several male friends, all of whom cook very well, got into a boasting match about their respective omelet prowess. One who is significantly younger than the others challenged the group to prove its worth. There immediately arose a serious contest between the upstart Kid and the venerable Champ. A neutral kitchen was chosen for the match, and several judges were easily recruited. The Great Northwest Omelet Bake-off was ready to begin.

The Kid arrived with the latest in equipment, recently acquired from his mother's specialty kitchenware shop. The Champ's pans and bowls had been around for years and had the definite look of tools of a master. Or so the judges thought before the Kid began to cook with his pan, which, although bright and shiny, was put expertly to use.

The first category was a classic cheese omelet, the second a vegetable montage. The Kid took the first round handily; his creation excelled in taste, texture, and general appearance. The Champ, however, made a strong comeback in the second round—squeaking by the Kid to take the honors in the vegetable category.

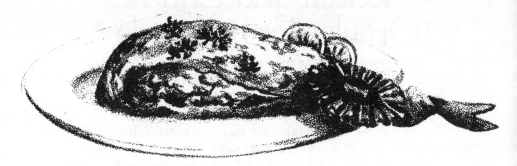

Finally, with the judges scarcely able to eat another bite, the freestyle match began. Each contestant had carefully kept his entry secret from the group. Although both were exceptional, age and perhaps wisdom ultimately prevailed, as the Champ won the third round unanimously. His freestyle omelet featured Dungeness crab, sour cream, and mango chutney, and was garnished with watercress, orange slices, and fuchsia blossoms!

One needn't be quite so committed to the art as the Champ and the Kid to make a dandy omelet in the kitchen, but a little enthusiasm certainly helps. In addition to good equipment, there are a few special hints that help ensure omelet success.

The eggs should be thoroughly beaten with a balloon whisk, preferably in a copper bowl, since sufficient air must be incorporated into them before they are poured into the hot pan. I find that the copper bowl speeds the beating process considerably.

As a rule, the smaller the omelet, the easier it is to handle. Two medium eggs should be allowed per serving with a modest amount of filling, especially until the art of turning the omelet is mastered.

The final caveats are to grease the pan sufficiently and to make sure that it is properly heated. A thin film of butter should coat the entire cooking surface, no matter how well the pan is seasoned. A well-prepared pan will cook an omelet perfectly in just a few minutes.

I use two methods of omelet preparation, depending on the kind of filling to be combined with the eggs. I find that grated cheese and thinner sauces, preserves, and chutneys work best with the French method. The so-called American method is great for lightly sautéed vegetables and chopped fruit used as filling.

–Cheddar and Chutney– Omelet, French Style

1 tablespoon butter
4 medium eggs, well beaten
¾ cup grated Tillamook
   or sharp Cheddar cheese
3 tablespoons green tomato chutney
¼ teaspoon salt
¼ teaspoon freshly ground black pepper

Melt butter in 10-inch omelet pan over medium heat. Add eggs when butter begins to bubble and let eggs set. Lift edge of egg mixture and let uncooked egg run underneath. Repeat once or twice until egg is dry. Sprinkle cheese over top and let it melt. Spread chutney over cheese, sprinkle salt and pepper over top, and fold. Serves 2.

–Vegetable Omelet,– American Style

3 tablespoons butter
1 small shallot, minced
1 medium green pepper, diced
½ small zucchini, thinly sliced
4 medium eggs, well beaten
½ teaspoon salt
¼ teaspoon freshly ground black pepper

Melt butter in 10-inch omelet pan and sauté vegetables until tender. Add well-beaten eggs, stir, and permit bottom of mixture to brown. Turn out onto plate and immediately return to pan with uncooked side down. Or turn omelet over with large spatula. Cook second side until toothpick comes away clean from center. Serves 2.

–Peach Melba Omelet

Sweet omelets are an Austrian favorite, but they are not often prepared in this country. Various fruits in season with a sprinkling of boiled raisins make an excellent filling. This recipe was a sudden inspiration several years ago and has since become a standard in my kitchen.

> 1 tablespoon butter
> 4 medium eggs, well beaten
> 3 ripe peaches, finely chopped and drained
> 3 tablespoons raspberry syrup
> 2 tablespoons confectioner's sugar

Melt butter and swivel to thoroughly coat bottom of 10-inch omelet pan. Pour well-beaten eggs into pan and cook over moderate heat, lifting edge occasionally as eggs begin to set. Repeat until eggs are dry and spoon peaches into center. Pour syrup over top, fold, and dust with sugar. Serves 2.

–Frittata

A frittata is an Italian variation of the French omelet. It also lends itself to the imaginative use and combination of numerous vegetables and herbs.

> ¾ lb. ground beef or sausage
> 1 medium onion, chopped
> 1 lb. fresh spinach, coarsely shredded
> ¼ lb. fresh mushrooms, thinly sliced
> ½ teaspoon sweet basil
> 8 medium eggs, well beaten
> Salt and pepper

In medium frying pan brown beef over moderate heat, then add onion and sauté until tender. Add spinach and mushrooms and stir occasionally until spinach begins to wilt. Beat eggs in separate bowl and add basil. Pour eggs into pan, stir once, and cover. Cook 5 to 8 minutes or until eggs set. Lightly sprinkle with salt and pepper. Serves 3–4.

–Crab-Asparagus–
Mushroom Quiche

Quiche, the easy-to-make French egg-and-cheese pie, offers another delicious way to combine fresh eggs with various vegetables, meats, and seafood. Although bacon, onions, and Swiss cheese are the traditional filling, quiche provides unlimited possibilities. Most garden vegetables are good in quiche, but asparagus, broccoli, and zucchini are especially tasty. Shrimp or crab are excellent additions, as are wild or domestic mushrooms. The cream-cheese crust is an old family favorite.

½ lb. asparagus, cut into 2-inch pieces
¼ lb. mushrooms, thinly sliced
½ lb. fresh Dungeness crabmeat, well cleaned
3 medium eggs
1 cup whole milk
½ cup heavy cream
1 cup grated Swiss cheese
½ teaspoon salt
¼ teaspoon granulated garlic or garlic powder

—Cream Cheese Crust —

4 oz. cream cheese, at room temperature
4 tablespoons butter, at room temperature
¾ cup flour

With a pastry blender, 2 knives, or one's hands, combine butter and cream cheese with flour until thoroughly mixed. Chill for 10 minutes and roll into single crust ⅛ inch thick. Put into quiche pan or 9-inch pie pan.

In large saucepan, steam asparagus until tender. Sauté mushrooms in medium frying pan until lightly browned. Distribute asparagus, mushrooms, and crab evenly over crust. Combine eggs, milk, and cream, then add grated cheese, salt, and garlic and stir until thoroughly blended. Pour this custard mixture into quiche pan and bake at 375° for 45 minutes or until top is brown and center is firm. Serves 6.

Waffles

Although soufflés, omelets, and quiche are often likely to turn up on the table at brunch or dinner, breakfast is the meal that means eggs. And not eggs simply scrambled or fried, but used in waffles, pancakes, and French toast as well. I often add an extra egg to any large waffle or pancake recipe for better nutrition, and I always serve the finished product with homemade jam, syrup, or marmalade.

—Beer Waffles———————

Waffles are a perennial favorite with people of all ages. This variation of a standard recipe makes a very light waffle, which is crisp on the outside and custardlike beneath the crust. The batter is quite thin and the beaten egg whites will float to the top after every filling of the waffle iron, so it is important each time to stir the mixture well before pouring.

> **2 cups sifted all-purpose flour**
> **4 teaspoons baking powder**
> **¼ teaspoon salt**
> **2 eggs, separated**
> **1½ cups milk**
> **1 cup flat beer**
> **½ cup butter, melted**

Mix dry ingredients. Then add milk and beer and beat until smooth. Add beaten egg yolks and blend thoroughly. Beat egg whites until stiff and fold into batter along with melted butter. Makes 4 large waffles.

PLANTING THE VEGETABLE GARDEN

One of the greater joys of any spring season is the planting of a backyard vegetable garden. Numerous enthusiasts in the Pacific Northwest, both country folk and city dwellers, make a space in their yard for seeds and starts. Some people restrict planting to cedar pots and boxes on an outdoor deck, but most actually spade up a nearby piece of ground. The city of Seattle has even organized a program of matching people with vacant urban lots, in order that those with little or no space of their own can plant a sizable garden.

My garden is in an apple orchard next to the neighbor's sheep pasture. The old trees form a natural clearing which is open to the sun from late morning until late in the afternoon. The site is large, potentially as much as half an acre, and well-defined by a blackberry thicket at one end and several apple trees at the other. It's a peaceful place, disturbed only by occasional traffic on the driveway several hundred yards away and the bleating of a momentarily discontented sheep.

There had been a garden on the same site several years earlier, but the weeds had grown back vigorously after the last vegetable had been harvested. The soil had become too depleted of the necessary nutrients and minerals to grow anything but weeds and field grass. It took several winter weekends and dozens of wheelbarrow trips between my chicken coop and the garden to get the soil ready for planting once again.

A plowman arrived one rainy Saturday morning, pulling a special rig designed to break even the most uncooperative sod. He worked quickly, and in twenty minutes, the knee-high grass was plowed under and the newly turned soil was ready for careful marking into hills and rows.

I had spent hours several months earlier poring over seed catalogues, talking to gardening neighbors, and dreaming about my crop. As beginners generally do, I was eager to try everything at least once and so had fashioned several different schematic drawings of where and how my garden would grow.

When the seeds arrived from mail-order nurseries throughout the country, I built a greenhouse of boards and sheet plastic to give the seeds a place to grow until they could be set out, as small plants, into the garden. I then sowed several flats of lettuce, spinach, broccoli, cabbage, and squash. With the heat of four 300-watt light bulbs at night and mild daytime temperatures of forty-five to fifty degrees, the seeds sprouted and grew quickly. The greenhouse by the way, was indispensable later in the season for growing eggplants, peppers, and tomatoes, which generally require a warmer climate to mature outdoors.

Some six weeks after sowing in flats, most of the seeds will have become plants that are anywhere from two to six inches tall. Some of those plants, such as lettuce and spinach, will mature within sixty days after being set into the garden soil. If conditions are warm and not too rainy, it is possible to have a home-grown salad on the dinner table by late June.

In the midst of all the preparation and planting in the spring, though, my garden always provides one early reward, gratefully received by both gardener and friends. Rhubarb in several perennial varieties flourishes in this climate—and especially well, it seems, in a particular corner of my garden.

Although I like the deliciously tart pink stalks simply steamed with raisins and brown sugar, rhubarb readily lends itself to more elaborate desserts. Its common name—pie plant—is no accident. A pioneer favorite, rhubarb pie is still eagerly anticipated on many Northwest tables as the first "fruit" pie of the year.

—Rhubarb Custard Pie——

Crust for unbaked 9-inch pie shell
2 cups rhubarb, chopped into 1-inch pieces
1 cup brown sugar
1½ cups light cream
½ cup water
3 eggs, lightly beaten
1½ tablespoons cornstarch

Roll out pastry and place in pie pan. Arrange rhubarb on bottom of shell and sprinkle half the sugar over top. Combine remaining sugar, cream, water, eggs, and cornstarch, and stir until thoroughly blended. Pour custard over fruit and bake at 425° for 10 minutes, then turn heat down to 350° for 40 minutes or until center is firm. Serves 6.

–Rhubarb Applesauce Cake

1½ cups brown sugar
½ cup butter, at room temperature
1 medium egg
1 cup buttermilk
2 cups all-purpose flour
1 teaspoon baking soda
½ teaspoon salt
1 teaspoon vanilla
1 cup applesauce
1½ cups rhubarb, chopped

Combine sugar, butter, egg, and milk, and stir until smooth. Sift flour, soda, and salt together, and add to milk mixture, stirring until thoroughly blended. Add vanilla and applesauce and stir until smooth. Fold rhubarb into batter and pour into greased square baking pan. Bake at 350° for 1 hour or until toothpick inserted in center comes out clean. Serves 9.

BACKPACKING IN THE OLYMPIC MOUNTAINS

Nothing attracts people from other parts of the country to the Pacific Northwest more than the opportunity for outdoor recreation within minutes of the major urban centers. Those who would spend a weekend or a month exploring the nearby mountains, find unlimited possibilities for wilderness backpacking, day hiking, and camping by car. Although car camping is often possible in some relatively remote locations, those who enter the high country on foot are most likely to find solitude and tranquility.

Backpacking can be as rigorous or relaxed as the hiker might wish. Although the basic needs of food, shelter, and warmth can be met with a modest amount of simple equipment, most overnight campers opt for more sophisticated sleeping bags, tents, packs, and stoves. In any season, warm rainproof clothing is essential, as is a pair of properly fitted waterproof boots. Once equipped, all the compleat backpacker needs for years of low-cost high-reward vacation enjoyment is a good map.

Both the Cascade and Olympic Mountains are riddled with trails, which often suffer from overuse, especially during high season. The mild climate west of the Cascades means that camping is possible almost throughout the year. The smart hiker heads out in the late fall, winter, or even early spring—months when even the most over-used trails are virtually empty.

One such area, far from the beaten path except during July and August, is the countryside surrounding the northern slopes of Mount Adams, which is located some seventy miles southeast of Mount Rainier. Over twelve thousand feet high, Mount Adams is one of a chain of formerly active volcanoes that dominate the landscape of western Washington and Oregon. Although it is covered with snow throughout the year, Adams, unlike its neighbor Mount Rainier, supports very few glaciers on its flanks. It is an easy target for novice mountaineers, and it is even the site of a community trek of some three hundred people of all ages along the southern side to the summit every August.

It is a long drive from the urban areas of Puget Sound through miles of heavily logged timber country to the head of the Mount Adams road. From Randle, a prosperous logging community, a well-packed gravel road winds through the Mount Adams Wilderness Area. The road heads gently uphill, past several small, picturesque lakes. There are occasional breaks in the thick forest that allow glimpses of the hills surrounding the mountain. Even in July, snow lingers on the shoulders of the road as a reminder of the brevity of the season during which man can explore this wilderness.

My friends and I planned to hike some ten miles, taking us a thousand feet above timberline and placing us high on the shoulders of the mountain. We would set up camp there for several days and then decide whether or not to attempt the summit. We were not compelled to reach the top of this mountain and would be quite content to enjoy the awesome tranquility of this elevation and the spectacular views of neighboring peaks.

The trail through the pine forest was quite narrow and rose gently at the outset. Each of us carried just over forty pounds of gear and supplies— enough to keep us in camp for four or five days. Although many campers resort to purchasing freeze-dried packages of food from local outdoor-equipment stores, we were stocked on this trip with a good selection of home-dried fruits and vegetables, whole grains, and a few tins of meat. All that we would need was a source of clean water to complete our menu for the next few days.

The wise backpacker puts a lot of time and energy into planning every meal, and then spends hours on advance preparation of necessary supplies. Since variety is especially important in trail-side cooking, it is best to carry small quantities of several different fruits and vegetables, for example, than several pounds of any single item.

A variety of spices and herbs is also essential, chosen carefully to enhance the seemingly endless procession of one-pot meals. Some of my favorites include curry powder, powdered garlic, oregano, basil, and chili powder.

A good homemade dryer, either a free-standing or stovetop model, will easily do the job of getting peaches, pears, apples, plums, apricots, bananas, and pineapple ready to pack. Quality control is assured, of course, when the preparation is done at home, and the cost of home-dried fruit is significantly less than that of the prepackaged varieties.

Vegetables also work well in a dryer, whether they are cut into large pieces or into thin slices to be used as flakes in cooking. Tomatoes, green peppers, and onions lend themselves especially to the flake method, and zucchini, green beans, mushrooms, and broccoli will stand up well in slices or larger chunks. All and any of these combine nicely with whole grains or noodles to provide a tasty and satisfying one-dish meal.

Fruits and vegetables selected for drying should be in good condition. Any bruises or other imperfections should be removed. Each item should be washed thoroughly and can be peeled if desired, although peeling is not necessary if the fruit or vegetable is carefully washed. Cut them into thin slices and place closely together, but not touching, on a dryer rack.

The racks, usually made from nylon screen in homemade dryers or perforated aluminium sheets in the commercial varieties, allow free circulation of warm air. When filled, the stovetop dryer should be placed over low heat. If the dryer is homemade, the heat source, usually a high-watt light bulb, should be activated. The slices on the top racks will dry faster than those below; so the unit must be checked frequently to remove the slices that are thoroughly dried and to rearrange those that are not. Fruit and vegetables with less moisture, such as broccoli and carrots, usually dry faster than wet ones, such as tomatoes.

Another save-time, save-space product that comes in handy on the trail is prepared baking mix, which simply needs the addition of an egg or water to become pancakes, biscuits, or dumplings.

Our party passed a rather primitive shelter, which, on closer inspection, turned out to be an early homesteader's cabin. A carpet of huckleberry bushes surrounded the old structure; it would be late summer before the fat, blue berries would be ready for harvest. We wondered what else that early settler had lived on, since the resident animal population seemed so scarce. We later discovered that deer run thickly in these forests, and bears occasionally turn up as well.

Although we had not been able to see the mountain for several miles, to-pographical evidence indicated that the timberline was approaching and that the view would soon be unimpeded. Evidence of long-ago volcanic and glacial action became more apparent and we began to notice steep scree slopes piled high with cinders and other volcanic debris. We were suddenly forced to walk around several deep gorges, presumably formed by the once great rivers of ice.

Toward sunset, we arrived on the shoulders of the mountain and pitched camp near a stream running from a giant snowfield. There were no trees or underbrush since we were far above timberline, but the ground was covered with a heatherlike plant that provided a great natural cushion for the tent and sleeping bags. The temperature dropped quickly as one of us set up the tent and the rest began to prepare supper.

–Chicken Curry–

An interesting and tasty variation of this recipe substitutes dried fruit, especially pears, peaches, raisins, and apples, for the chicken.

4 cups water
2 cups bulghur wheat
2 tablespoons cooking oil
2 chicken bouillon cubes
1 teaspoon curry powder
2 tablespoons tomato flakes
1 tablespoon onion flakes
4-oz. can cooked chicken
½ cup raisins
½ cup walnuts, pecans, or pine nuts

Put water in large pot and add bulghur, oil, bouillon, curry powder, tomato flakes, and onion flakes. Bring to a boil and simmer for 20 minutes. Add chicken, raisins, and nuts and cook for an additional 5 minutes. Serves 2.

—Spanish Ala————————————

Another one-pot meal features bacon or hard salami, which can only be transported in small tins if expected to keep more than a day or two away from a refrigerator. On a relatively long trip of a week or more, hikers often arrange food drops or caches in order to limit packweight, as well as to vary their diet. This recipe makes a good cache.

¼ lb. bacon or hard salami, chopped
2 cups brown rice
4 cups water
1 beef bouillon cube
1 small can tomato paste
½ teaspoon chili powder
1 tablespoon dried onions

In large pot fry bacon or salami until brown. Pour off most of the grease, add rice, and fry lightly. Then pour in water with bouillon cube and bring to a boil. Reduce heat and simmer for 20 minutes.

Add tomato paste, chili powder, and dried onions, and cook for 5 more minutes. Serves 2.

—Vegetarian Noodles————

Chinese egg noodles offer a welcome change from precooked rice or bulghur and are especially filling. Different vegetables can be used in this recipe each time it is served.

1 quart water
2 packages Chinese egg noodles
  with seasoning packet
2 eggs, lightly beaten
½ cup dried mushrooms
2 tablespoons dried onions
½ cup dried green peppers
½ cup tomato flakes

Boil water in large pot and cook noodles according to package directions. Add seasoning packet included with noodles, eggs, mushrooms, and other vegetables. Stir and simmer for 3 minutes. Serves 2–3.

–Sausage Glop——————

Cheese can be added to this or any of the previous one-pot recipes for variety and good taste. Sausage Glop, despite its somewhat unfortunate name, is a particularly delicious one-pot meal, guaranteed to satisfy even the hungriest hiker.

2 cups rice
1 tablespoon margarine
4 cups water
1 package mushroom soup mix
1 can Vienna sausages, sliced,
   or ½ lb. hard salami, sliced
1 teaspoon dried parsley
½ lb. jack cheese, cubed

Combine rice and margarine in water and bring to a boil. Add soup mix, sausage, and parsley, and simmer for 20 minutes. Remove from heat and add cheese, covering for several minutes to let cheese partially melt. Serves 2–3.

–Biscuit and Pancake Mix——

Prepared baking mix is well worth its weight for hungry hikers who want morning pancakes or dinner biscuits. Almost any combination of whole-grain and white flours is acceptable, but one backpacking enthusiast I know uses a totally whole-grain mixture of whole wheat, rye, and corn meal. The combination should be packaged carefully in an airtight container, as any moisture will quickly spoil the flour. Nine 3-inch biscuits or four 6-inch pancakes can be made from this recipe. The amount of mix can be multiplied, of course, if a bigger breakfast is desired.

1 cup all-purpose flour
   or ½ cup all-purpose flour
   and ½ cup whole wheat flour
½ cup rye flour
½ cup yellow corn meal
2 teaspoons baking powder
1 teaspoon salt
1 teaspoon baking soda
3 tablespoons brown sugar

Mix all ingredients thoroughly. Makes about 2½ cups. Use a traditional pancake or biscuit recipe, substituting mix for everything except egg, water or milk, and oil.

—Beef Jerky——————————

Organized meals are often few and far between on the trail. In addition to dried fruit, sunflower seeds and roasted soy beans make great snacks or light lunches. I also like to carry a homemade supply of beef jerky, which is simple to prepare and very satisfying. I use lean round steak, although just about any lean cut of beef will do.

2 lbs. round beefsteak
1 tablespoon salt

With a very sharp knife, cut salted beef in thinnest possible strips, cutting with grain. Place slices on oven rack and bake at 150° for 8 to 16 hours. Leave oven door slightly ajar and test jerky every hour to achieve desired texture. *Note:* Place cookie sheet under rack to catch drippings.

Trail Fare

I use broken pieces of jerky in my version of gorp, the trail food that most hikers carry, which always seems to turn out a little differently each time it is made. The salty meat I usually include provides a tasty foil for the rest of the ingredients which are usually sweet. Some of my favorite makings for gorp include dried banana and pineapple chips, shredded coconut, yellow raisins, walnuts or filberts, and chocolate or carob chips. This energy-giving snack is easy to carry in a convenient pocket for periodic munching.

Homemade nut butters are another nutritional and delicious treat to carry on the trail. My favorite nut butter combines raw Spanish peanuts with grated orange rind, sunflower seeds, honey, and nonfat milk solids. The nuts and seeds should remain fairly chunky. Outdoor-equipment stores sell convenient plastic tubes, which can be filled at one end and sealed and squeezed through the other end onto pilot biscuits or smaller crackers. These tubes are also good for carrying jam or honey.

SPRINGTIME PICNICKING

Although ten of the Puget Sound ferries in the present fleet have been built and put into use since the state took charge of the system in 1951, some of the original vessels that first sailed in the early days of the service are still hard at work. Built in the 1920s and 1930s and often used in other waters before coming to Puget Sound, these older ferries are as romantic as they are practical, complete with plush leather seats, brass railings, and glass-protected observation decks.

All of the ferries are used daily by commuters and tourists alike. Some provide Puget Sound islands with their only link to the mainland and others save hours of travel time to points west and north of Seattle. The most popular runs command the newest, largest, and fastest boats, but the less heavily traveled routes, such as the one to the San Juan Islands, still employ the more nostalgic members of the fleet.

The day was gray, and a light mist rose slowly from the water. We had left the mainland shortly before noon; in less than thirty minutes the ferry was preparing to dock at its first small port. A few cars were driven off, some passengers walked on board, and the boat backed away from the slip and sailed on to the next stop. There were four destinations on this run, so my friends and I had plenty of time to enjoy the picnic lunch we had packed for the trip.

Although the ferry system leases a food concession on each boat, there is little food from the galley that is tempting. Most passengers, especially those who plan to eat an entire meal while traveling, bring along a basket filled with delicious treats from home.

I usually let my imagination run wild when packing a picnic for such ex-cursions. Two or three salads are standard, as are homemade bread and a couple of good desserts. This particular voyage, prelude to a much antici-pated weekend, brought out some of my best picnic creativity.

–Curried Eggs

6 eggs, hardboiled, peeled, and halved
1 teaspoon cider vinegar
⅛ teaspoon curry powder
¼ teaspoon salt
¼ teaspoon pepper
Dash dry mustard
3 tablespoons mayonnaise
**   or sour cream**

Separate egg yolks from whites and combine with rest of ingredients. Stir until smooth and spoon yolk mixture into whites. Makes 12.

–Edisto Island Meatloaf

1½ cups bread crumbs
1½ cups milk
3 lbs. ground beef
***or* 1½ lbs. beef *and* 1½ lbs. sausage**
3 eggs, lightly beaten
2 large garlic cloves, mashed
½ cup finely chopped onion
2 teaspoons salt
1 teaspoon oregano
1 teaspoon dried parsley
1 tablespoon Worcestershire sauce
½ teaspoon Tabasco sauce
⅓ cup red wine

Soak bread crumbs in milk. Add meat, eggs, garlic, and onion, and mix well. Add salt, oregano, and parsley. Pour in Worcestershire sauce, Tabasco sauce, and wine, and blend thoroughly. Form into large loaf or two small loaves and place in long baking pan. Bake at 350° for 45 minutes. Serves 6.

—Mac's Mother's Mustard—
Sauce

½ cup dry mustard
½ cup cider vinegar
1 egg
⅓ cup sugar
Dash of salt
1 cup mayonnaise

Place mustard and vinegar in jar with tight-fitting lid, stir well, and let stand overnight. In top of double boiler, combine mustard mixture, egg, sugar, and salt, and cook until thickened, stirring constantly. Cool and stir in mayonnaise until well blended. Makes approximately 2 cups.

—Kim Chee

1 medium Napa cabbage,
  coarsely shredded
2 tablespoons salt
3 scallions, cut into 1½-inch pieces
  and shredded lengthwise
3 garlic cloves, minced
1 teaspoon grated ginger
1 teaspoon chopped red chili pepper

Sprinkle cabbage with salt, mix well, and let stand for 15 minutes. Then wash cabbage in cold water and combine with scallions, garlic, ginger, and chili pepper, and mix well. Put into a stoneware crock or glass jar and add enough water to cover. Let stand for at least two days before serving. Serves 6.

—Rice Salad

2 cups cooked rice
6 pitted green olives, chopped
1 small carrot, peeled and diced
½ green pepper, diced
2 scallions, chopped
3 tablespoons olive oil

1 tablespoon tarragon vinegar
1 small garlic clove, mashed
½ teaspoon salt

Combine rice, olives, and vegetables, and mix well. In separate bowl mix oil, vinegar, garlic, and salt. Stir well and pour over rice. Serves 4.

–Marinated Tomato Salad

2 large tomatoes, thinly sliced
1 medium onion, thinly sliced
1 cup ketchup
1 tablespoon sugar
1 tablespoon cider vinegar
1 tablespoon olive oil
1 teaspoon dried basil
1 small garlic clove, mashed

Place tomatoes and onion slices in bowl in alternating layers. Combine rest of ingredients, mix well, and pour over top. Let stand at least 2 hours before serving. Serves 4.

–Anadama Bread

1 tablespoon dry yeast
2 cups warm water
¼ cup molasses
1½ cups corn meal
1 cup wheat germ
1 cup whole-wheat flour
2 teaspoons powdered orange rind
½ cup toasted sesame seeds
1 tablespoon salt
4 tablespoons oil
2 cups whole-wheat flour
2 cups unbleached flour

In large bowl dissolve yeast in water. Add molasses and stir until blended. Pour in corn meal, wheat germ, 1 cup whole-wheat flour, and orange rind, and beat for 100 strokes. Then add sesame seeds, salt, oil, and remaining flour, and combine as much as possible. Place dough on well-floured board and knead into smooth satiny ball, using more flour to absorb moisture so dough is not sticky.

Let dough rise in warm place until double in bulk, punch down, and form into two small loaves. Place loaves on baking sheet in warm place and let rise until double in bulk. Bake at 375° for 50 minutes or until crust darkens.

–Cheese Straws

½ cup butter, softened
1 lb. grated sharp Cheddar cheese
1¾ cups all-purpose flour
½ teaspoon salt
¼ teaspoon cayenne pepper

Blend butter and cheese, add flour, salt, and pepper, and blend to form smooth dough. Roll dough wafer-thin and place on greased baking sheet. Cut into narrow strips 4 inches long. Bake at 350° for 25 minutes or until lightly browned. Makes about 100.

–Good Old Brownies

1½ cups brown sugar
¾ cup melted butter
1 egg
3 tablespoons cocoa
1 teaspoon salt
½ teaspoon baking soda
1½ cups all-purpose flour
½ cup sunflower seeds,
    walnuts, or pecans

Beat sugar into butter, add egg, and beat until creamy. Then add cocoa and stir until well blended. Mix salt, soda, and flour together, and add to butter mixture, stirring until smooth. Spread into greased square baking pan, sprinkle with seeds or nuts, and bake at 375° for 20 minutes.

SUMMER

Cooking with concern for seasonal abundance characterizes not only many of the best private kitchens in the Pacific Northwest, but also a number of popular restaurants in Seattle, Portland, and other nearby areas. Steak and lobster houses no longer monopolize the commercial market, and restaurants of diverse and ambitious ethnic orientation open almost weekly. Among the most imaginative and well-received new ventures are those featuring the seasonal specialties of the Pacific Northwest.

The choice of fresh produce, seafood, and fruit is never greater than during the warm months of summer. Bright skies and moderate temperatures combine to create a fantastically productive growing season for vegetables and some fruits west of the Cascades. East of those mountains, the summers are hot and dry, but massive irrigation from the Columbia River allows growers in the Yakima Valley to produce the fruit, vegetables, and hops that distinguish this fertile region.

Summer is also the peak season for clams, even though these mollusks are available for gathering almost any time of year. Minus tides which expose large stretches of beach and mild weather seem to provide particular encouragement for those who gather clams. Fishing, too, becomes more popular during the summer. Bottom fish are always present in Puget Sound, but in the late summer and early fall, the salmon are at their peak, returning upstream from the ocean and inland waters to spawn in the rivers of their birth.

Kitchens in the Northwest hum with excitement during the summer months. What is fresh at the grocery, at roadside stands, and in backyard gardens often determines the daily menu. Both professional chefs and great cooks at home pay close attention to seasonal bounty and often they head to the Pike Place Market.

PIKE PLACE MARKET

The "low stalls," as they are known, fill quickly on Saturday mornings with farmers who bring their produce into town from the southern end of the county. The "high stalls" are more permanent installations, replete with local fruit and vegetables, as well as much from California and Mexico. Several fish and meat markets do a brisk business, as do the cheese sellers and delicatessens. Craftspeople have regular booths, street music can be heard from early morning to late at night, and the crowds come daily to the Pike Place Market, one of the few urban farmers' markets still thriving in an American city.

In 1907, a Seattle city ordinance established the market on a waterfront site in the downtown area to give local farmers a place to sell directly to consumers. By 1911, nearly three hundred thousand shoppers a month were attracted to the bustling area. A residential community, mostly made up of waterfront workers, sprang up around the market, and as a result dozens of small businesses opened their doors. Clothing, hardware items, and household goods of all description were suddenly available right next to the stalls of dairy products, meat, fish, and produce.

By the late 30s over 550 farmers were selling at the market. But that was the height of the area's popularity, which declined in the 40s and 50s with the advent of shopping centers and suburban sprawl. It wasn't until about ten years ago that the market again became a fashionable place to shop, and even then there was much serious discussion of tearing down many of the deteriorated facilities and building new hotels, apartment buildings, and a huge downtown parking garage.

But a group of citizens, who saw the market as an irreplaceable urban resource, formed a committee and began a public campaign to save it. A local ballot initiative was approved in 1971 which required the city to preserve the existing market area and renovate and improve the buildings. This community—which among other accomplishments had inspired Mark Tobey to draw his famous Market Sketches—*would be allowed, indeed encouraged, to survive.*

*The resulting improvements have made the market more of a city asset
than ever before. The residential character of the area has evolved to include middle- and upper-income residences, side by side with the dwellings
of the earlier residents whose income is fixed and very limited. Dozens of
new shops and services have opened in the last two years, right next to the
older more established businesses. There are thrift shops, antique stalls,
flea markets, barber shops, a garden center, and several pornography out-
lets in addition to the specialty food shops and stalls of all kinds.*

*Predictably, three of the best city fish markets call the market their home.
"Send a Salmon East" suggests one, as it wraps dozens a week in plastic
bags and dry ice for a trip across the country. Another boldly claims to
have the largest selection of available seafood in the Northwest. Several
large glass cases hold dozens of trays of fillets, steaks, and chunks of fish,
as well as a lot of cleaned and processed shellfish. In front of the display
cases, though, are bins piled high with seafood—different kinds of salmon
and other fish, geoduck and butter clams, mussels, prawns and shrimp,
squid and octopus, occasionally abalone, local scallops or smelt, and
dozens of Dungeness crab.*

*Seafood is a market specialty, but fruit and vegetables from local farmers
fill many stalls as well. The Pike Place market is a giant outdoor grocery store
that draws thousands of shoppers every day.*

SUMMERTIME FRUIT

*Fresh fruit is essential in any kitchen devoted to seasonal bounty,
whether it is a classy Seattle restaurant kitchen or one's own work area at
home. And fortunately for those of us in the Pacific Northwest, much of the
nation's fresh fruit is grown locally. Collectively known, to the trade at
least, as "soft fruit," pears, peaches, sweet cherries, prune plums, and
apricots from Washington and Oregon are among the best in the country.*

*The Yakima Valley in south central Washington is the center of this culti-
vated abundance, followed closely by sections of central and southwestern
Oregon, where major river valleys such as the Rogue and Umpqua account for a large share of the regional fruit production.*

*Although pears come into season during the fall and winter, most of the
other soft fruit is brought fresh to market during the summer. Peaches, for
example, are almost always available in July and August at roadside
stands, both east of the mountains where they are grown and to the west,
where most of the peach-eating population lives.*

The important peach varieties in the Northwest are Red Haven, Elberta, and Hale. Generally available in grocery stores from May through late October, store-bought peaches often have the fuzz on their skins mechanically removed by the processors—on the theory that smooth skins make peaches more attractive to the shopper. Peach lovers think that is all rather silly, of course, and many will intentionally seek out the small roadside stands in order to buy fuzzy fruit.

Sweet cherries are also an important Northwest crop, especially in Oregon and also in British Columbia. Royal Anne, Bing, and Lambert are the major varieties, and they are shipped for eating fresh from May through August. Apricots and prune plums account for the rest of the commercial Northwest fruit crops, although their production is somewhat limited by smaller market demand.

Any soft fruit is probably best when eaten right off the tree, but since that is not a possibility for most of us, any homemade pie, cobbler, or tart has to be close to the perfect dessert when made with fresh fruit. But in my view, the ultimate use for fresh fruit is as an addition to homemade ice cream.

Fruit added to an ice cream mixture should be finely chopped. If cut into large pieces, the fruit will freeze harder than the ice cream and create undesirable lumps.

My freezer has a hand crank, and, depending on the enthusiasm of those present, we can have ice cream for ten—about half a gallon—ready to eat after 45 minutes of steady cranking. It is important to regulate the temperature around the bucket with plenty of rock salt in order to ensure proper freezing. If two cups of rock salt are added to the ice used in a standard freezer (an 8:1 ratio of ice to salt), the melting process will be controlled and the ice cream frozen to perfection.

–Homemade Peach–
Ice Cream

I used the cooked-custard method of making ice cream for years, until I recently discovered this much simpler method that requires no cooking and halves the preparation time.

The fruit, in this instance peaches, is cut into chunks and then mashed with a pastry blender to create some juice, a lot of pulp, and few small pieces.

> **5 eggs**
> **2½ cups sugar**
> **¼ teaspoon salt**
> **2 cups whipping cream**
> **2 cups light cream**
> **1 13-ounce can evaporated milk**
> **3⅔ cups whole milk**
> **2 tablespoons vanilla**
> **3 cups mashed peaches**

Whip eggs, sugar, and salt until fluffy. Then add cream, milk, vanilla, and fruit. Pour into bucket in center of freezer and churn for 35–45 minutes, making certain to keep ice full to top of bucket and mixed with 2 cups rock salt. Serves 8–10.

–Fresh Peach Tarts–

These peach tarts are spiced and flavored with ginger and Cointreau. Fresh raspberries or strawberries may be substituted for the peaches.

> **Pie dough for double-crust pie**
> **4 cups sliced fresh peaches with juice**
> **¼ cup Cointreau**
> **2 teaspoons fresh grated ginger**
> **Whipped cream *or* yogurt for garnish**

Pinch off walnut-size pieces of dough, roll out and cut into 4 inch circles. Shape over inverted muffin-tin cups and prick each with fork. Bake at 425° until golden brown, about 3–4 minutes. Gently pop off shells and cool them.

Fill each tart shell ⅓ full of peaches, soaked in liqueur and ginger. Garnish with unsweetened cream or yogurt and serve. Makes 18 tarts.

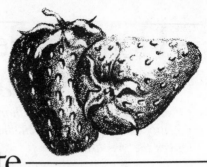

—Fruit Compote

*Peaches make an excellent condiment served with most meat and fowl.
This fruit compote can be easily varied to feature fruits in season or even
made from dried fruits when necessary. The longer it bakes at low temperature, the better it tastes when served.*

½ cup fresh pears, sliced
1 cup fresh peaches, sliced
½ cup pineapple, cut into chunks
1½ cups applesauce
1 teaspoon cinnamon
½ teaspoon powdered ginger
½ teaspoon nutmeg
Juice of ½ lemon
Rind of ½ lemon, finely chopped

Combine pears, peaches, and pineapple with applesauce, and arrange in
square baking pan. Mix cinnamon, ginger, and nutmeg, and sprinkle over
top. Sprinkle lemon juice and rind on top. Bake at 250° for 1 hour. Serves 6.

—Marsala Peaches

*This simple wine marinade turns an ordinary peach into a piquant condi-
ment. Any sweet wine will work well.*

6 large fresh peaches, halved
1 cup Marsala *or* other sweet wine
2 cinnamon sticks, broken into 1-inch pieces

Place peach halves in shallow bowl and cover with wine. Top with
cinnamon-stick pieces and let stand at least overnight, longer if possible.
Serves 3–6.

—Fresh Fruit Drinks———

Combinations of different fruit flavors are marvelous and very healthful. Fruit drinks have recently gained great commercial popularity in the Northwest and many people try making their own at home. The results can be as simple as a single fruit and ice or as interesting as several different fruits, yogurt, and wheat germ blended together.

Some of these concoctions are called smoothies, a perfect description of their rich and mellow texture, and others are labeled slurps, for the quiet way in which they are usually consumed.

Combine any of the following in a blender and whirl until smooth. Slightly overripe fruit often provides the best results. Try—

Peaches	**Plums**	**Raspberries**	**Cantaloupe**
Apples	**Bananas**	**Strawberries**	**Papaya**
Blackberries	**Melon**	**Oranges**	

If more liquid is required, add milk, orange juice, or ice cubes. For an unusual treat, try a few fresh mint leaves tossed into the blender along with the fruit.

For a meal in a glass, include yogurt, cottage cheese, milk, or ice cream along with the fruit.

—Apricot Milkshake———

Fresh fruit drinks are wonderful, but they can never replace the good old milkshake for me. This healthy variation of the old drugstore favorite soothes my guilt as well as my palate.

6 very fat, ripe apricots
1 cup milk
1 cup large-curd cottage cheese
Juice from ½ orange

Pit apricots and combine with other ingredients in blender. Whirl at high speed and serve chilled. Makes 1 serving.

–Apricot Stuffing––––––––

A variation on more traditional fruit and bread stuffings, this apricot-and-soy stuffing goes very well with pork and lamb, as well as with chicken or duck.

½ cup green pepper, chopped
½ cup onion, minced
3 tablespoons butter
1½ cups fresh apricots, chopped
3 cups cooked buckwheat groats
or brown rice
Freshly ground black pepper
4 tablespoons soy sauce

In medium frying pan, sauté green pepper and onion in melted butter. Add apricots and grain. Grind pepper over top to taste and moisten with soy sauce. Makes 5 cups.

–Chicken and Cherries––––––

Sweet cherries are usually eaten out-of-hand or flambéed for cherries jubilee. But cherries are also delicious when baked with pork or chicken.

1 frying chicken, cut into pieces
1 cup flour
½ teaspoon salt
¼ teaspoon black pepper
¼ teaspoon paprika
Oil for cooking
½ cup Marsala *or* sweet vermouth
1 cup pitted sweet cherries
¾ cup sour cream

Put flour, salt, pepper, and paprika in brown paper bag. Put chicken pieces inside bag, one at a time, and shake each piece thoroughly until covered with flour. Heat cooking oil in large frying pan and cook chicken until lightly browned.

Place chicken in long baking pan and pour in wine. Bake at 375° for 15 minutes. Remove from oven and add cherries. Return to bake for another 15 minutes or until chicken is golden brown and pulls away easily from bone. In last 5 minutes of baking, spread sour cream over top of chicken and mix well with cherries. Be careful not to overheat (and curdle) sour cream. Serves 4.

WILD AND DOMESTIC BERRIES

Although peaches, pears, and cherries from the Pacific Northwest have established a national reputation of excellence, the berry crops are an important resource. The mountains are full of wild berries, which helped sustain the Indians and early pioneers. These huckleberries, blackberries, strawberries, and elderberries, as well as other lesser known varieties, supply seasonal kitchens in the Northwest today. The summer berry season means days of intense culinary activity.

Most of the wild fruit is eaten within a few miles of the bush where it grew, but both raspberries and strawberries are major commercial crops in the western counties of Washington, Oregon, and British Columbia. These berries are shipped by the truckload to grocers throughout the country.

One center of strawberry cultivation lies some sixty miles north of Seattle on the Skagit Flats—a peaceful delta formed by the Skagit River as it rushes down from the Cascades on its way out to northern Puget Sound. This is lush farm country, divided into quarter sections nearly a hundred years ago by pioneers. The land was then mostly marsh, so a system of dikes was built to reclaim it from its swampy origin. Fertile fields were soon being worked and record crops of oats and hay were grown here in the early days.

Many of the original farms have been broken into smaller parcels, where bulbs, seeds, and vegetables are now grown. This is a quiet corner of the Pacific Northwest, interrupted only by activity at LaConner, a prosperous fishing village and home to a number of well-known Northwest artists.

Strawberries

Despite wet winters and other hardships, a warm May and June will result in the production of sweet and perfect strawberries. So for a few weeks in the early summer, much of western Washington goes slightly strawberry mad.

Strawberry season is usually at its peak in backyard gardens as well by the Fourth of July. The holiday is celebrated by dozens of Northwest towns with parades, barbecues, fireworks, and, of course, strawberries. On

Bainbridge Island near Seattle, the town of Winslow hosts one of the most lively festivals of all.

Town fathers have decreed Winslow the Puget Sound center for an old-fashioned Fourth, and everyone in three counties is invited to join the fun. Site of the major ferry depot between Seattle and the Olympic Peninsula, Winslow is certainly accustomed to crowds, but not quite like those that come to celebrate the Fourth every year.

On Main Street, dozens of booths are manned by craftspeople, Boy Scouts, and members of the Ladies Aid. One booth boasts a dunking stool, another offers a game of chance. There's a pie-throwing contest across the street, next to a quilt-and-dollhouse raffle. People stand shoulder to shoulder for several blocks, chatting with friends, spending money, and planning the rest of the day's activity.

About noon, however, the street suddenly begins to clear, and places along the sidewalk and on top of buildings are assumed by all. It's time for the parade, an event which draws as much or more attention than the fireworks later that evening. For this isn't just a small gesture of civic pride, it's a procession of kids and bands and animals and beauty queens and yacht-club officials and old cars and fire engines and literally anyone around who wants a chance to march.

And march they do; as a result the parade is usually several hours long. My favorite act of all is a group of aging former high-school musicians known as the West Bainbridge Nearly Philharmonic Marching Band. Some forty different "musicians" strut down Main Street with lots of different instruments, playing the same two songs over and over and over. One song sounds vaguely patriotic, but the other is clearly a Christmas carol. And this motley crew gets its inspiration, I am told, from the gallons of fresh strawberry daiquiris consumed earlier in the day.

—Fresh Strawberry—
Daiquiris

1 cup strawberries
½ cup crushed ice
4 oz. light rum
1 tablespoon lime juice

Combine ingredients in blender and whirl for 20 seconds on high speed. Add sugar or honey to taste (this is only necessary if the berries are not fully ripe). Serves 2.

—Strawberry Cheese Pie—

To vary this easy and delicious pie, make it with a graham cracker crust.

Baked 9-inch pie shell
4 oz. cream cheese, softened
4 cups fresh strawberries
1 cup sugar
3 tablespoons cornstarch
Whipped cream

Stir cream cheese until very soft and spread on bottom of shell. Place half the berries on the cheese. Mash the remaining berries—which should then measure about 1½ cups, including juice. In medium saucepan, bring fruit to a boil over medium-high heat, then add sugar and cornstarch. Let boil for 1 minute and cool. Pour over berries in shell and chill for several hours. Garnish with whipped cream. Serves 6.

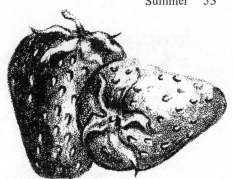

–Strawberry Soup–

One bright July day, one of my favorite local restaurants greeted lunch customers with colorful bowls of chilled strawberry soup. Unusual and quite tasty, strawberry soup can be served as the first course for a light luncheon or for brunch.

2 cups fresh strawberries
3–6 tablespoons sugar
1 cup chicken stock
½ cup sour cream *or* crème fraîche

Purée berries in blender and add sugar to taste. Strain through very fine sieve, then add chicken stock and blend thoroughly. Stir in sour cream or créme fraîche, chill, and serve. Serves 4.

Raspberries

Rasberries follow strawberries in the harvest season and are grown commercially throughout western Washington on small farms. Backyard raspberries almost grow themselves and require very little care. A good stand of raspberries will produce fruit for ten to fifteen years. I have found that twenty bushes more than meet my yearly needs for jam, sauce, and shortcake—and raspberries are my favorite berry.

—Raspberry Sour—
Cream Shortcake

Strawberry shortcake is good, but I think raspberry shortcake is even better. Topped with crème fraîche or slightly sweetened sour cream, raspberry shortcake is an elegant, simple summer dessert. This particular version can be baked in individual servings or all together in a shallow baking dish or pie pan. If baked whole, be sure to test for doneness by inserting a toothpick into the center—when toothpick comes out clean, shortcake is done.

3 cups all-purpose flour
½ teaspoon salt
4 teaspoons baking powder
1 tablespoon sugar
½ cup butter
1 cup milk
4 cups fresh raspberries
1 cup sour cream, sweetened to taste,
   ***or* 1 cup crème fraîche**

Mix dry ingredients together and cut in butter with pastry blender until texture resembles corn meal. Add milk and stir until mixture forms soft dough. Knead for 2 minutes on floured board. Press dough into bottom of 9-inch pie pan and bake at 400° for 25 minutes or until top is brown. Cut into wedges and serve warm with berries and sour cream on top. Serves 6.

Berry Jam

I suppose that some would call it lazy and others a waste of precious freezer space, but I have finally decided—after years of standing over the stove—to make berry jam simply by freezing. First of all, it is a very quick and easy procedure, and second, the berries retain enough of their original shape to give the finished product more substance than when they are cooked and sealed into jars for pantry storage. I can do an entire flat of fruit this way in much less than an hour—to make a similar quantity of cooked jam takes about three times as long.

Freezer jam requires no cooking. It does demand liquid pectin, which aids jelling, and fresh lemon juice, which enhances the flavor. But it's easy to incorporate some natural pectin in the mixture. Simply include some green berries in the bucket with those that are ripe.

–Raspberry– Freezer Jam

4 cups raspberries
2 cups sugar
2 tablespoons lemon juice
3 ounces liquid pectin

Crush some berries, leaving 1 or 2 cups whole. Add sugar and mix thoroughly. Combine lemon juice and pectin and add to fruit. Stir for 3 minutes until most of the sugar has dissolved. Pack in plastic containers, or in clean freezerproof glass jars (leaving an inch of headroom), and freeze immediately. Makes about 3 pints.

Blackberries

Blackberry vines begin to flower in July, and by mid-August the fruit appears. The lovely little wild ones—often half the size of their domesticated cousins—are usually earlier. Many country restaurants boast homemade wild blackberry pie in the late summer. But even if they are exaggerating a bit about the origin of the berries (wild ones are somewhat scarce), a piece of fresh blackberry pie is well worth a stop on a trip home from the ocean or mountains.

Backyard blackberries seem to need more sunshine than other fruits to ripen to perfection. A weed in almost everyone's opinion, blackberry canes often cover steep hillsides and abandoned roads. Regardless of their lowly lot, the berries produced during a sunny summer are as big as marbles and absolutely delicious.

—Blackberry Upside-down Cake

2 cups blackberries—wild if possible
½ cup butter
½ cup white sugar
¾ cup brown sugar
1 egg, lightly beaten
1 teaspoon vanilla
1½ cups whole-wheat flour
1 teaspoon soda
1 teaspoon baking powder
½ teaspoon salt
1 cup sour cream or milk

Wash and drain berries. Reserve ¼ cup brown sugar. Cream remainder with butter and white sugar until light. Add egg and vanilla and stir vigorously. Sift dry ingredients together and add to butter mixutre alternately with sour cream or milk. Spread fruit over bottom of greased long baking pan. Sprinkle with reserved sugar and pour in batter. Bake at 350° for 35–45 minutes or until cake is done in center. Serve warm with whipped cream or ice cream. Serves 6.

—Blackberry Punch

Although this blackberry punch is sure to turn your teeth a bit blue, it makes an unusual, tasty drink. Serve with or without vodka or brandy.

4 cups blackberry juice
2 cups orange spice or other spicy tea
2 whole cloves
2 whole allspice

Cinnamon stick
Lemon peel

Cook about 8 pints of blackberries over low heat to yield 4 cups juice when vigorously mashed. To obtain juice, wring pulp through cheesecloth and then set aside to drip into bowl.

Mix juice and tea and add cloves, allspice, and a 2-inch piece of cinnamon stick. Simmer over low heat for 3 minutes and serve with a strip of lemon peel in each cup. Makes 10 servings.

Blueberries

An unusually sunny summer will ripen both wild and domestic blueberries by August, but September is usually the peak of the season. These berries thrive in the acid soil of rainy western Washington and grow to great size when lightly fertilized.

Blueberries have been cultivated only for the last fifty years, which is probably why many recipes still call for wild fruit. Valued not only for their tasty fruit, blueberries make a striking ornamental hedge displaying white blossoms in the spring and crimson foliage in the fall.

—Blueberry—
Sour Cream
Pancakes

1⅓ cups unsifted all-purpose flour
½ teaspoon baking soda
1 teaspoon salt
1 tablespoon sugar
1 egg, lightly beaten
2 teaspoons oil
1 cup milk
1 cup sour cream
1½ cups blueberries
4 tablespoons melted butter

Combine dry ingredients and add egg, oil, and milk, stirring well. Fold in sour cream and blend mixture until smooth. Gently add blueberries, stir, and drop batter by spoonfuls onto hot buttered griddle. Makes 10 medium-sized pancakes.

–Blueberry Crackle Cake–

Nutmeg and blueberries are a delicious combination. Ground cloves are a good substitute for the nutmeg.

2½ cups all-purpose flour
½ teaspoon salt
1 cup sugar
4 teaspoons baking powder
1 teaspoon nutmeg
⅓ cup shortening
1 egg, lightly beaten
1¼ cups milk
1 cup fresh blueberries

Mix dry ingredients and cut in shortening. Add egg and milk and stir well. Fold in fruit and bake at 375° for 40 minutes in greased square baking pan. Serves 9.

–Wild Blueberry Muffins–

Wild blueberries are a special treat well worth the day or two of purposeful effort required to fill several gallon jugs. I like to head up to the mountains on a bright late-summer day, carry a large plastic sack or two, and spend the afternoon picking—and eating—as much fruit as I can find. What is brought home from those excursions is usually gone within a week, but it's an especially delicious week, full of hot muffins in the morning and pie or cake at night.

2 cups whole-wheat flour
1 teaspoon salt
3 teaspoons baking powder
½ cup brown sugar
2 eggs
1 cup milk
2 tablespoons oil
1½ cups wild blueberries

Combine dry ingredients with fork. Separate eggs and beat whites until peaks form. Beat milk, yolks, and oil together, and quickly add dry ingredients, combining with a few brisk strokes. Carefully fold in beaten egg whites and then add fruit. Fill greased muffin cups ⅔ full. Bake at 400° for 15 minutes or until brown. Makes 12 muffins.

CLAMS AND MORE CLAMS

July often boasts those hot, bright, radiantly clear mornings that inspire most of us to be up and out and ready for an adventure. On one such occasion four able-bodied souls gathered large plastic buckets, sturdy shovels, and a pitchfork or two and headed down to the beach with a promise to return with dinner. The tide was ebbing quickly; at its lowest point more than 120 feet of graveled beach would be exposed. The conditions were ideal for clamming, and, with a little good fortune and concentrated endeavor, the buckets would be filled in less than an hour.

Nearly every beach in Puget Sound nurtures a share of clams, whether within major city limits or way out in the country. All of the Sound beaches were once laden with this edible resource, but today those that are in public domain are fairly well depleted of much marine life. Private beaches, though, just minutes from major metropolitan centers, regularly boast six to eight steamers to the shovelful of sand, and a bucket can be filled almost as quickly as the gatherer can dig.

Although there are some thirty different species of clams currently thriving in Puget Sound, there are only three or four types that attract most diggers. At the top of the list are native little-neck and butter clams, both small and succulent and highly prized as steamers.

A shovelful of sand dug below the mean tide line yields a number of curiosities, some edible, some not. Clams appear in various sizes, from one to six inches in diameter. Included in the shovelful, too, are usually some beach "shrimp" (actually small crayfish), an occasional worm, and often a hermit crab. The beach shrimp can be used in a seafood stew, but ordinarily the clams alone are kept for eating.

In addition to steamers, many beaches also yield larger clams. Often called horse clams, these are in fact full-size butter clams and little necks. Then there are geoducks (pronounced gooeyducks), the largest of all clams that abound in the waters of western Washington. Virtually ignored by all but a few of the initiated for many years, geoducks are now being harvested and marketed in great numbers, mostly to Japan.

Although digging clams requires nothing more than a token amount of equipment and a strong back, there are certain things to consider before tossing the clam into the bucket. Most important, the clam must be alive, which is easy to determine: a live clam, when disturbed, will quickly pull its neck into its shell and spit water. Closed shells should be closely inspected to see if they are ''mudders'' —shells filled only with sand. Such shells will usually come open if sideways pressure is exerted on both the top and bottom with a finger and thumb.

When digging for steamers, another consideration is size. Most people like steamed clams that are no more than two inches in diameter. If the spot you are digging yields mostly larger clams, it is likely that someone has been there first, and you should either try elsewhere or plan to make chowder.

There is no need to dig deep in order to find steamer clams, since they usually live six to eight inches below the surface. I think a pitchfork is the most efficient tool for digging. One plunge with a regular-size pitchfork removes enough sand and gravel to uncover the clams. The sand falls quickly through the tines as the fork is lifted, and the clams can be easily spotted. Any trenches or holes you make should be refilled with sand to encourage the growth of young clams in the same spot.

Once the buckets are filled—and I find that twenty to thirty clams feed one person if steamers are to be the main course—the next step is cleaning. I have tried several different methods and find that the simplest and most effective means is to fill the bucket with sea water, put it in the shade, and let it rest for several hours without disturbance. The clams will clean themselves of sand and debris rather quickly and then need only an additional rinse with fresh water and a scrub brush to be ready for the top of the stove.

Although I have steamed clams on the beach in a pit fire covered with seaweed, it is really a lot more satisfactory to use a large pot with a tight-fitting lid and place it on the stove or over a well-tended campfire. The container allows the juices to make nectar as the clams cook. Most clam freaks treasure the nectar nearly as much as the clams themselves, especially if it is well seasoned.

–Steamed Clams

**5 dozen little-neck or butter clams
1 large onion, peeled and quartered
2 garlic cloves, lightly crushed with fork
½ cup chopped parsley**

Pour 1 quart of water into a large pot. Thoroughly rinse clams and set aside. Add onion, garlic, and parsley to water, and bring to a rolling boil. Toss in clams and reduce heat to low. Steam clams for 12 to 15 minutes, or until all are open. Pour off nectar and serve separately. Serves 2–3.

–Island Clam Chowder

Good chowder recipes come out of most seasonal kitchens and are a real culinary landmark in the Pacific Northwest. This particular version came from one such kitchen that regularly feeds groups of ten to thirty hungry guests on weekends throughout the summer. The island cook reports that "this is an especially good way to entertain and feed mainland guests. They will not only dig the clams and peel the potatoes, but will work up a great appetite in the process and be especially eager to feast on the results of their efforts." The important thing in this chowder is to use lots of fresh tarragon and freshly ground black pepper.

**1 quart water
2 garlic cloves, minced
6 dozen clams, 1–3 inches in diameter
3 tablespoons butter
2 cups onions, coarsely chopped
8 slices bacon *or* ½ lb. salt pork, diced
6 cups chicken stock
6 cups potatoes, peeled and diced
1 bay leaf
½ teaspoon ground thyme
¼ teaspoon allspice
2 teaspoons salt
½ teaspoon black pepper
2 tablespoons fresh tarragon
8 cups milk
3 tablespoons flour
½ cup clam nectar**

Pour water into a very large pot, add 1 garlic clove, and bring to a boil. Add clams, reduce heat, and steam for 15 minutes or until all clams are open. Remove clams from shells, mince, and set aside. Reserve nectar. Nectar not required below can be served separately with meal.

In large frying pan melt butter and sauté onions, remaining garlic clove, and bacon or salt pork until onions are soft. Pour off fat and put mixture into large soup pot or the clam steamer. Add stock, potatoes, and seasonings. Bring to boil and simmer for 15 minutes, or until potatoes are tender, but firm.

Add clams and milk to soup and cook over medium heat for 15 minutes. Combine flour with nectar and stir until smooth. Add to chowder, stirring until chowder thickens and bubbles for 1 minute. Serves 10–15.

–Clam Sauce I

There are rarely any remaining steamers after they are served for dinner, but when there are, I like to make an herbed spaghetti sauce the next day. This sauce freezes well and is a great midwinter reminder of summers on the beach.

2 tablespoons butter
1 cup water
1 medium shallot, minced
½ teaspoon salt
1 bay leaf
1 quart clams, coarsely chopped or ground
½ cup dry vermouth
Freshly ground black pepper

In medium frying pan melt butter and sauté shallot until soft. In medium saucepan bring water to a boil, add salt and bay leaf, and simmer for several minutes. Then add clams, shallot, vermouth, and pepper, and simmer 5 minutes more. Serve over spaghetti or other thin pasta. Serves 4.

–Clam Sauce II

Leftover steamers just won't do for sauce in some kitchens where the cooks insist that clams used for cooking should always be raw. Large raw clams are excellent in the following sauce.

Large clams must be gutted and cleaned a bit differently than steamers. With a sharp knife, open the clam by inserting the tip of the knife blade between the two shells at the base. Then sever the adductor muscle that holds the clam shut. Run the knife underneath the clam until the entire body is freed from the shell. Remove the gray stomach, discard it, and reserve the rest. The best eating comes from the neck or siphon, breast, and "foot" or the adductor muscle.

> **3 tablespoons butter**
> **3 tablespoons flour**
> **2 cups milk**
> **1 cup light cream**
> **1 quart clams, chopped or ground**
> **1 medium onion, finely chopped**
> **and lightly sautéed**
> **Few sprigs of fresh parsley, torn**
> **Fresh tarragon, coarsely shredded**

In medium saucepan, melt butter, stir in flour, and cook for several minutes over low heat, stirring constantly. Add milk and cream and stir until mixture begins to thicken. Then add clams, onion, and herbs, and simmer for 15 minutes, stirring well. Serves 4.

—Baked Clams——————

When I finally tire of chowder and steamers and pasta, which despite my firm resolve to the contrary seems to happen every year, this idea is always good for a few more clam dinners

> **6 large clams, steamed, cleaned, and ground**
> **(reserve broth from steaming)**
> **6 strips bacon, cooked, drained and crumbled**
> **1 egg**
> **½ cup cracker meal**
> **Freshly ground black pepper**
> **2 strips raw bacon, cut into thirds**

Mix clams, crumbled bacon, egg, and cracker meal together, using enough broth to moisten. Fill single clam shells with mixture, sprinkle with pepper, and top with piece of raw bacon. Place under broiler for 7 minutes. Serves 2.

Razor Clams and Geoducks

Although gathering steamer clams requires a modest amount of digging, there are those clams that demand both great strength and perseverance to get them out of the sand and into a bucket. Pacific razor clams, considered to be an outstanding delicacy by many, are one such species. Located on the broad sand beaches washed by the Pacific Ocean in Washington and Oregon, razor clams provide great sport for the estimated 300,000 hopeful harvesters who head out to the ocean every winter and spring.

These three- to five-inch specimens are able to dig through the sand and thus escape their pursuers. Special equipment helps catch these clams, as do good eyes and a strong back. First of all, the digger has to spot a "show," which is the small dimple in the sand that gives away the clam's position. The trick is to plant a clam gun, an ordinary shovel, or even a length of stovepipe just six inches seaward of the show and then dig quickly to catch the diving clam. Dry digging, which is done in the summer, is best for beginners, while winter surf digging brings out the experts. The sand is more fluid in the winter, which provides these slippery creatures an even better chance to escape.

Much the same equipment is used for the recreational harvesting of geoduck. Largest of our clams, geoduck average three pounds, but have been known to tip the scales at a beefy thirteen! Geoduck are legion on the bottom of Puget Sound and along the coastal bottoms off British Columbia as well.

Commercial harvesting of geoduck has been popular in the past few years. Divers, working at depths of twenty to seventy feet, dig the clams from the bottom with jets of water from hand-held hoses. By grabbing the neck, which will retract when disturbed, and then shooting a blast of water around it, the diver works the clam loose from its home one to four feet under the sand. A diver must bring up four hundred clams a day to make good wages, but the better workers can haul as many as a thousand from the bottom during a single shift.

The state of Washington leases the clam beds to commercial harvesters and closely monitors the catch. Yet few Puget Sounders treat geoduck as

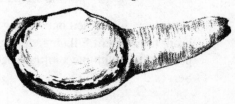

an edible natural resource, so most of the harvest is shipped directly to Japan, where geoduck is highly prized. Part of the reason that geoduck have been ignored at home is that, until recently, the only way to get one was to dig it yourself.

Geoduck are only uncovered on beaches during the very lowest tides of the year and even then are usually found mostly in spongy tidal mudflats. A two-inch indentation or "mark" in the sand will almost surely mean that a geoduck is hiding under the surface. The digger must first find the neck of the geoduck, which is directly below the "mark," and then center a stovepipe over it. The stovepipe is then driven into the sand as deeply as possible and the fun truly begins. The neck is held with one hand and the other scoops sand away from it, making a large hole in the process. Unlike razor clams, geoduck do not move their bodies when disturbed. Once the neck is grabbed, if the diggers are persistent, they will always get their clam! When the body of the clam is reached, often two and sometimes as much as four feet below the surface, the geoduck can be lifted out of the hold. This chose and capture actually works better with two or three people at work—a single digger must be extremely agile and tenacious to get even one of these clams.

Geoduck are strange-looking creatures, since their bodies are substantially bigger than their shells. The entire clam is edible—neck, breast, and stomach. Breast meat tastes more like abalone than clam, and the stomach is a special delicacy.

Geoduck should always be brought into the kitchen alive, not only to ensure freshness, but to minimize the toughness from rigor mortis.

Cleaning a geoduck is simple: A knife is run between the body and the shell to separate them, and the clam is then scalded in hot water to remove the thick skin from the neck. If live geoducks are frozen, though, the neck skin will fall off easily and muscle tissues will relax as the clam thaws. After the skin is removed, the stomach should be separated from the breast meat.

The neck can then be cut in half lengthwise and chopped into four pieces. The breast may be cut into four large pieces. If possible, the meat should then rest for an hour. Then all pieces may be pounded vigorously with a mallet until the muscle tissue feels relaxed, although some experts maintain that this step is unnecessary, particularly for the tender breast pieces.

–Geoduck Steak–––––

Geoduck steak should be cooked quickly in very hot oil. One good cook I know says the oil must be smoking; others use thermometers to measure 400°.

1 live geoduck, cut into 4-inch steaks

½ cup whole-wheat flour, *combined with*
½ teaspoon thyme *and* **salt and pepper**

or

2 eggs, lightly beaten, *combined with*
1 cup cracker crumbs *and* **salt and pepper**

Oil for frying

In large frying pan heat oil to 400°. Dredge steaks from neck and breast in either of above mixtures and fry until golden, usually about 4–5 minutes. Serves 6.

–Marinated–––––
Geoduck

Marinated raw geoduck is elegant, flavorful, and very heathful. Try different combinations; I like this soy and ginger marinade.

2 geoduck breast pieces, unpounded
½ cup soy sauce
¼ cup lemon juice
1 teaspoon freshly grated ginger
2 garlic cloves, minced

Cut breast pieces into ⅛-inch strips. Combine soy, lemon juice, ginger, and garlic, and pour over clam strips. Add more juice if strips are not entirely covered. Marinate 30 minutes. Serves 6.

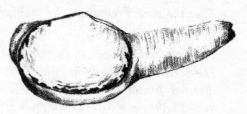

—Duck Soup

*Geoduck stomachs have the same qualities as good sweetbreads. They
have different summer and winter characteristics, as a result of the ab-
sence or presence of plankton in their diet. The digested algae is replete
with nutrients, and it tastes good too.*

**2–3 geoduck stomachs
4 tablespoons butter
2 garlic cloves, minced
1 cup thinly sliced celery
3 scallions, chopped
2 cups whole milk
Salt and pepper to taste**

Carefully slice stomachs into bite-size chunks and sauté gently in medium
saucepan in butter and garlic. Add celery and scallions and stir to blend.
Add milk, salt and pepper, and simmer gently over medium heat for 20
minutes. Serves 4.

SALMON

*The alarm rang just after dawn, and, as I started to turn over for another
hour's sleep, I remembered why the bell had sounded so early. It was the
beginning of a bright sunny morning at Nahmint Bay Lodge, a fishing resort deep in the interior of Vancouver Island, and I had come for several
days to try my luck. Hundreds of king salmon were waiting to head upriver
and were swimming cautiously in the bay beside the river's mouth. With a
modicum of good fortune and a small amount of skill, I hoped to land my
daily limit of one in the quiet cool hours before breakfast.*

*Fishing resorts and daily charter-boat services are both popular in the
Northwest. Although five different species of salmon thrive there, only
three provide sport-fishing opportunities. Usually around twelve but as much
as forty pounds, mature Chinook, also known as king or tyee, are the
prizes—and these were the ones I was fishing for that August at Nahmint.*

*In a remote spot, accessible only by seaplane or boat, the lodge is made
up of four log buildings, carefully constructed nearly fifty years ago, and
secured at the water's edge on logs used as floats. One side of the bay has
been pretty well logged, but the other still boasts stands of virgin Douglas
fir and cedar. Bear and cougar often visit the lodge in the winter, and
birds of all description make stops nearby on their migratory flights. Much*

*of the surrounding countryside is still wilderness, as yet unspoiled by en-
croaching timber companies or crowds of people.*

*Chinook salmon leave the ocean and return to their native river to spawn
when they are four or five years old. During this activity, they are often
found in deep water close to shore, and in areas where tides and currents
capture smaller bait fish, such as herring. Although they are not actually
feeding just before they spawn, they will be attracted to properly set lures
and bait. Relatively heavy fishing gear is needed to land a big Chinook, in
addition to a fairly long line. Both tackle and instructions are provided at
a resort like Nahmint, which makes fishing there especially attractive to
novices.*

*With our lines all but baited, my fishing partner and I headed out into the
bay in a small aluminum skiff powered by a small motor. We moved slowly
across the water and expectantly let out the lines as instructed by the lodge
manager, an expert fisherman himself. Just as we reached the other side of
the bay, my partner got a strike. Several nearby boats kept their distance
in order to avoid tangling our active line. The fish broke the surface and
then dove, pulling hard on the line. But my partner continued to reel him
in carefully for the next thirty minutes and finally shouted to me to grab the
landing net as the fish neared the boat. I leaned out and scooped up the
fish with a surprisingly graceful motion.*

*We excitedly headed back to the lodge, eager to weigh and show off our
triumph. By now it was 8 A.M. and a breakfast of eggs and pancakes,
sausage, and smoked salmon was waiting. Our fish, which weighed a re-
spectable twenty-two pounds, disappeared to be cleaned and made ready
for travel while we ate. It had been a fine morning!*

*Second only to apples—and clearly first in some circles—salmon are the
Pacific Northwest. It seems that just about everyone who lives here tries
his or her hand at catching a share of this carefully cultivated resource.
Most, happily, are successful.*

*All salmon are anadromous, which means that they are hatched in fresh
water, descend to salt water to grow to maturity, and return to the streams
of their birth to spawn and die. Spawning fish change color from their
lifelong silver to various shades of red, brown, and black. They also develop a hooked snout and a pronounced ''razor back.'' Spawning occurs
in gravel beds where the females bury their eggs. All Pacific salmon die
after spawning.*

*Chinook salmon are highly prized not only for their size and sport value,
but also for the taste and texture of their firm, dark pink flesh. There are*

Chinook in Washington streams and rivers from February through November, but the major spawning migrations occur in late spring, summer, and fall.

Coho, commonly known as silver salmon, averages only eight to ten pounds, compared to twenty or twenty-five for Chinook, but are also heavily fished both commercially and recreationally. Spawning migration usually occurs in September and October, and silvers are taken in great numbers from coastal rivers, Puget Sound, and the Columbia River.

A bit smaller fish than the coho on the average, the pink or humpback salmon is the most abundant of all. It is generally fished in odd years in Washington, and even-year runs occur in British Columbia and Alaska in the months of August and September.

Neither sockeye, nor chum (or dog salmon) get much attention from local anglers. Chum, which weigh ten to twelve pounds when mature, are caught by the commercial purse seiners and gill netters in Puget Sound and on the Columbia River in the late fall. The sockeye run in the summer months and are primarily headed for the Fraser River in British Columbia, as well as for the Columbia. These fish are valued for their bright red flesh, which has the high oil content and firm, even texture that makes it ideal for the canning industry.

Needless to say, salmon sustained man in the Pacific Northwest long before the "discovery" of Puget Sound. Fish, and especially salmon, were boiled, broiled or barbecued, steamed, dried, and smoked by most of the Indian tribes between the Cascades and the Pacific, as well as by those along the coast in Canada. Eaten fresh as long as possible and then dried and smoked for use during the rest of the year, salmon was a staple of that day and time.

Broiling, roasting, or barbecuing was accomplished by lashing a fillet onto several stakes which were then driven into the ground at an angle close to the fire. The fish could cook slowly on both sides this way. Sometimes the fish was steamed, New England clambake style, using hot stones and seaweed. Hot stones were also used to heat water held in cedar boxes into which dried fish was put to boil.

Preservation of most food, and especially salmon, was then a matter of drying. The fish was cut with mussel shells into strips and hung over racks in the sun or by a fire. Often the curing was done inside a long house, and smoking was part of the process. British Columbia Indians packed salmon roe into seal bladders and smoked them into something the pioneers laughingly called "Siwash cheese."

When the first white settlers came to the Willamette Valley in Oregon in the 1840s, they were astonished by the abundance of the region and quickly learned to include most of the local fish, shellfish, and game in their diets, especially until their gardens and domestic animals began to thrive. Reports from those days repeatedly mention the gratitude of the early settlers for the natural plenty around them.

The preparation of salmon for the table takes some planning and careful attention. Although very few cooks actually encounter a fish right off the hook, it seems appropriate to explain the basic method of preparing a whole fish for the pan.

There are different opinions on the necessity of scaling a whole fresh fish before cooking. I often do so myself by running the fish under cold water and working against the natural lie of the scales with a sharp knife. But many fish chefs never scale the catch at all, with no adverse effect on the finished product.

To remove the innards, a cut should be made from the anal vent to the head of the fish. Usually the entrails are neatly packaged in a pouchlike membrane, so that removing them from the flesh is not a messy task. If the fish is to be cooked whole, the pectoral fins and gills on the lower side should be removed and discarded, although small fish are often only gutted before being cooked. In either case, the entire carcass should be thoroughly rinsed in cold water after cleaning.

If steaks or fillets are desired, a bit more cutting is required. A large fish can be cut into ½- to ¾-inch steaks by cutting cross-sections along the body beginning just below the "collarbone." Fillets are the sides of the fish removed as a piece—so there are two fillets to a fish. Fillets can be obtained by cutting along the backbone from the tail to the head. The knife, which should be very sharp, is held flat along the ribs. A succession of small cuts is made until the entire length of flesh can be easily freed from the bone.

The way the fish is cut should be determined by the way it is to be cooked and served. There are six basic methods of preparing salmon, or any other fish, for the table. Each has its advantages and all are delicious, as long as the cardinal rule of good fish cookery is maintained: Do not overcook fish. Its delicate flesh requires relatively little cooking time, and fish will continue to cook even after it has been removed from the heat—for as long as the flesh remains hot.

The quickest way to prepare and serve salmon is to broil it under moderately high heat (375°–400°) for five to eight minutes on each side. Both

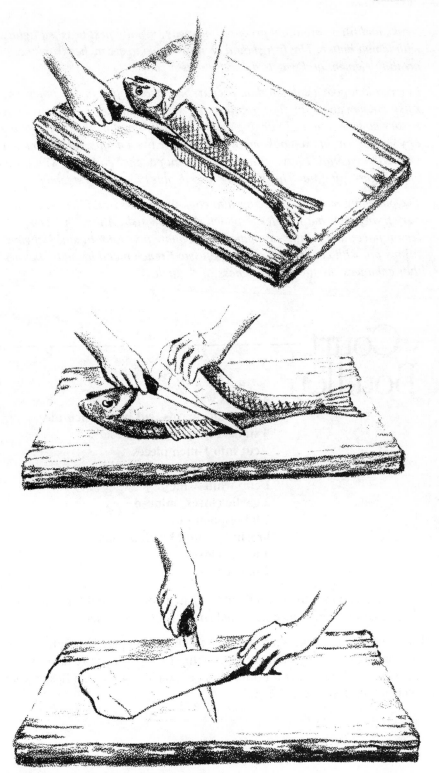

*steaks and fillets are often prepared this way, usually first brushed lightly
with lemon butter. The fish should be placed two to six inches from the
broiling element and watched carefully as it cooks.*

*I more often poach salmon than prepare my favorite fish in any other way.
I like the moistness the flesh retains after several minutes of simmering in a
savory court bouillon. Poaching is an especially good method for cooking
any whole fish, but to cook one weighing over five pounds, a fish poacher
is nearly essential. I have a large French tin poacher complete with a rack
and a tight-fitting lid. This poacher also doubles as a clam steamer.*

*The poaching method can be used to cook fish steaks and fillets in an ordi-
nary frying pan, but I prefer to poach the whole fish. Although water,
lemon juice, and a little salt make an adequate poaching liquid, I always
fill my pot with court bouillon, that classic French blend of subtle flavors
that enhances the natural goodness of the fish.*

–Court Bouillon

For a 5-lb. fish:
4 quarts water
2 medium carrots, cut into 1-inch pieces
4 stalks celery, with leaves,
 cut into 1-inch pieces
2 lemons, thinly sliced
1 cup white wine
2 garlic cloves, minced
1 tablespoon salt
Freshly ground black pepper
4 whole cloves
2 bay leaves

Put all ingredients into poacher and bring to a boil. Let boil for 5 minutes,
add pepper to taste, reduce heat, and simmer for 20 minutes.

If poacher has no rack, wrap fish in cheesecloth and place it carefully in
pot, making sure that bouillon covers entire fish. Cook gently in simmering (never boiling) water for 5 minutes per pound or until fish flakes when
touched with fork. Serves 6–8.

–Steamed Salmon

Salmon can be steamed by wrapping the fish as for poaching and placing it on a rack above a pot filled with boiling water. The pot should be covered tightly and the fish allowed to steam for twelve to fifteen minutes per pound. This method works well for steaks and fillets and guarantees that the flesh will remain moist.

–Baked Salmon

Baking is the most common method of salmon preparation and certainly one of the easiest. A whole fish can be baked either with or without stuffing. I like the taste of an olive-oil-and-garlic baste brushed liberally over the entire fish. Wrapping the fish with aluminum foil seals in the baking juices.

**5-lb. fresh salmon
3 large onions, thinly sliced
2 lemons, thinly sliced
½ cup olive oil
2 large garlic cloves, mashed**

Wash salmon thoroughly and pat dry. Line baking sheet with aluminum foil and place ¾ of onions and lemons on top. Stuff cavity of fish with remainder of onions and lemons and place fish on foil. Mix olive oil and garlic and brush over fish. Fold edges of foil over top and ends of fish and seal. Bake at 400° for 15 minutes per pound or until flesh flakes when touched with fork. Serves 4–5.

–Gravlax

In addition to the four basic methods of cooking fish, there are two other ways of preparing salmon that are especially important and commonly used throughout the Northwest. One is gravlax, or pickled salmon, a Scandinavian method with an end result somewhere between lox and pickled herring fillets.

Any good-sized fillet will do nicely for gravlax. A large ceramic, enamel-ware, or glass bowl or dish is needed for curing. Gravlax is wonderful when served with onion slices, gherkins, and melba toast for lunch or as hors d'oeuvre.

1 2-lb. salmon fillet, skin intact
⅔ cup sugar
⅓ cup salt
2 tablespoons dill seed
1 bunch fresh dill

Cut fillet crosswise into two large pieces. Mix sugar and salt together and rub completely into fish. Place one piece skin-side-down in enameled dish and sprinkle with 1 tablespoon dill seed and cover with several sprigs of dill. Cover with other piece of fillet skin-side-up and sprinkle with remaining dill seed and sprigs. Place heavy plate or weight on top of fish and leave in refrigerator for 3 days. Turn twice a day and baste with liquid that forms around fish. Serves 6.

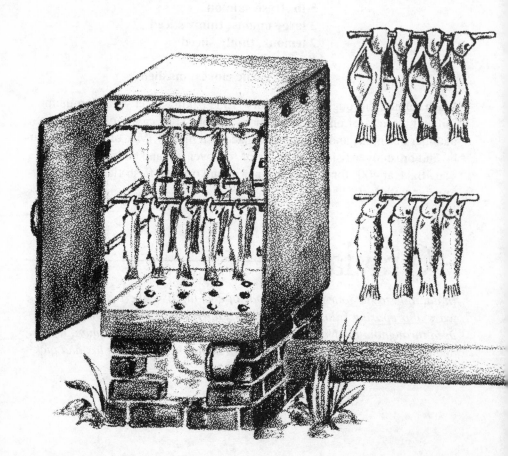

Smoked Salmon

The secret of good smoked salmon is not only in the brine. The outcome also depends upon the methods used to dry and smoke the fish. Successful smoking is done in a controlled smokehouse, which is often no more than an old refrigerator or oil drum. Salmon can be either "hot smoked," a process that cooks as well as smokes, or "cold smoked," one that only smokes.

One cold-smoking technique I know of calls for the firebox to be at least nine feet away from the smoker. A length of sturdy pipe is used to connect the two. To prepare the salmon for smoking, it should be immersed over-night or for twelve hours in a salty brine made up of 1⅔ cups of salt to four quarts of water. The salt should be completely dissolved in the water—a bay leaf or two may be added—and then the fish, cut into four-inch pieces, should be placed in a clean stoneware crock filled with the brine. (The amounts called for here will accommodate about fifteen pounds of fish.)

After removal from the brine, each piece should be lightly rinsed and then set out to dry, preferably outside in a shaded, well-ventilated place for at least two hours. This drying helps form the pellicle—the glassy, firm sur-face that permits the smoke to be absorbed and flavor the fish. Drying also helps ensure keeping quality; the drier the fish, the longer it will remain edible.

The dried fish is next put into the smoker on racks, a fire of green alder or other smoke-producing wood is built, and the door is shut for twelve to fourteen hours. After smoking for this length of time, the salmon will be well flavored and ready to eat.

Sauces for Salmon

Whether poached, broiled, baked, or steamed, even the most superb salmon can be notably enhanced by a sauce. This collection includes my favorites, which have been chosen after years of experimentation. Some are better with baked salmon, others are better with broiled. Most are delicious with other fish as well. Some will be immediately recognized, but maybe not so easily mastered, and others were simply invented out of curiosity and/or necessity.

—Lemon Parsley Sauce—

½ cup butter
1 tablespoon fresh lemon juice
1 small garlic clove, mashed
¼ cup chopped parsley

Melt butter in small saucepan and stir in lemon juice, garlic, and parsley. Blend well and stir over low heat for several minutes. Makes approximately ½ cup.

—Bercy Sauce—

2 tablespoons butter
1 tablespoon shallots, minced
¼ cup white wine
¼ cup fish stock
½ cup velouté sauce
2 teaspoons softened butter
1 teaspoon chopped parsley

Melt butter in small saucepan and sauté shallots until golden. Add wine and fish stock. Simmer until volume is reduced by half. Beat in velouté sauce, soft butter, and parsley. Serve warm. Makes 1 cup.

—Velouté Sauce

6 tablespoons butter
6 tablespoons flour
4 cups fish stock
1 small onion, peeled
1 whole clove

Melt butter, add flour, and cook, stirring constantly, over moderate heat for 3 minutes. Add fish stock and bring to a boil. Then add onion stuck with clove and simmer over low heat for 1 hour. Remove onion and serve. Makes 2 cups.

—Hollandaise Sauce

I have made a lot of curdled hollandaise sauce, and so a few words of advice seem appropriate on this most popular of all salmon sauces.

Proper equipment is important. I use a glass double boiler which ensures the conduction of gentle even heat. I also find a wire whisk indispensible in blending the ingredients carefully and evenly.

Hollandaise also demands a definite order of combining the ingredients. This sauce has a life of its own and will surely fail if the cook does not play by its rules. Finally, the water temperature over which the sauce is cooked must be moderate—bubbling, but not fully boiling—from beginning to end of the process.

3 egg yolks
3 tablespoons boiling water
½ cup melted butter
1½ tablespoons fresh lemon juice
slightly heated

In top of double boiler, place egg yolks and beat well with whisk. Add 3 tablespoons boiling water one at a time, stirring well after each addition until yolks thicken. Stir lemon juice into butter in small saucepan, then pour mixture very slowly into egg yolks, stirring constantly until smooth. Makes ¾ cup.

–Mayonnaise and– Capers

Mayonnaise is a great base for cold fish sauces. All sorts of greens and herbs can be mixed with it.

**1½ cups mayonnaise
2 tablespoons capers
1 tablespoon caper juice**

Mix ingredients thoroughly. Makes 1½ cups.

–Green Sauce–

**½ lb. spinach
4 sprigs parsley
1 cup mayonnaise
1 teaspoon fresh lemon juice**

Wilt spinach and parsley in boiling water, drain, and let stand for 5 minutes. Dry thoroughly and press through very fine sieve or grater. Blend with mayonnaise and lemon juice. Makes 1 cup.

–Cucumber Dill Sauce–

Cucumber dill sauce is a favorite on cold poached salmon.

**1½ cups yogurt
1 teaspoon honey
1 teaspoon dill weed
1 bunch scallions, finely chopped
1 large cucumber, thinly sliced**

Mix yogurt and honey. Add dill, scallions and cucumber. Stir until thoroughly blended. Makes 2 cups.

–Sour Cream Curry– Sauce

Try this on broiled salmon fillets.

¼ cup apple cider
2 cups sour cream
2 teaspoons curry powder

Pour apple cider into sour cream and stir until blended. Add curry powder and stir. Makes 2 cups.

–Vinaigrette Sauce–

This classic vinaigrette may well be the best salmon sauce of all.

2 egg yolks
2 tablespoons Dijon-style mustard
2 tablespoons shallots, finely minced
1 teaspoon salt
1 teaspoon white pepper
1½ cups olive oil

Mix all ingredients except oil and beat with whisk until thoroughly blended. Drizzle in oil, beating constantly, until well blended. Makes 2 cups.

BOTTOM FISH

Although salmon are surely our best-known native fish, dozens of other fish inhabit the ocean and the inland waters of the Pacific Northwest. Of the three hundred or more varieties living in the coastal waters of Washington alone, only about fifty can be successfully brought to the table from the hook on a fisherman's line. These fish are collectively known as "bottom fish," and they can be caught by anyone who has a small boat, proper fishing gear, and a bit of patience. Many bottom fish make excellent eating, despite their public image as only second-class compared to salmon.

The common names for several of the most popular bottom fish have been borrowed from similar (though biologically unrelated) species living in other waters. These names may be of interest to those who have eaten the real thing elsewhere and so expect the same texture and flavor from Pacific Northwest fish. The so-called sole of Washington waters is really flounder, and local red snapper is actually red rockfish.

Some of the best of the local bottom fish are the different soles (flounders), whose tender white flesh lends itself perfectly to the very simplest preparation. These fish are easily recognized by their flat bodies and by their eyes, both of which appear on the same side of the head. Normally, the ''eyed'' side is colored to blend with the fish's surroundings and the blind side is gray or white. These are true bottom fish—their entire adult lives are spent on the bottom of the sea.

The petrale sole is the most valuable of all and is a major commercial fish on the West Coast. It is often found in waters too deep for sport fishing, but is sometimes caught by salmon anglers using herring as bait, especially in the summer—when the sole migrate to shallower waters.

Careful attention to the preparation of bottom fish is essential. Perfectly cooked snapper or sole is unforgettable, whether it is broiled and basted with lemon butter or cut into bite-size chunks and tossed into a savory stew. The secret is not to overcook the delicate flesh.

—Wine-Baked Fish——

This simple wine-and-butter baste brings out the delicate, distinctive flavor of almost any Washington sole or flounder.

1 large onion, sliced
1½–2 lbs. fresh sole fillets
¾ cup dry white wine
1 teaspoon tarragon
2 cups mushrooms, thinly sliced
4 tablespoons melted butter
Salt and pepper to taste

Lightly grease long baking pan and put layer of onion slices on bottom. Place fish on top, pour in wine, and sprinkle tarragon evenly over fish. Cover with mushrooms and pour butter over top. Bake at 350° for 25 to 30 minutes. Sprinkle lightly with salt and pepper before serving. Serves 4.

Halibut

Pacific halibut is a prominent commercial fish that supports a large fleet operating from ports in Washington, British Columbia, and Alaska. Although male halibut may weigh as much as forty pounds at maturity, females can reach the awesome size of five hundred pounds. Since the texture of the larger specimens can be undesirably coarse, the most popular catch is known as chicken halibut, which weigh about ten pounds each.

—Skewered Halibut————

Halibut is highly prized as an eating fish, because of its firm white flesh. It is especially good when cut into small chunks, put onto skewers, and broiled over a charcoal fire.

> **2 lbs. halibut, cut into 1-inch cubes**
> **¼ cup lemon juice**
> **1 garlic clove, mashed**
> **¼ cup olive oil**
> **¼ cup soy sauce**
> **¼ cup dry sherry or sake**
> **½ lb. mushrooms, halved**

Combine all ingredients except fish. Put fish into ceramic bowl and pour in marinade. Cover and let stand for 30 minutes. Alternate fish cubes and mushrooms on skewers and broil for 10 minutes, turning and basting with marinade. Serves 4.

Rock Fish

Rockfish make up another major family of fish in Northwest waters, and some forty different species live in Puget Sound alone. Most of these fish have spines along the back that can inflict painful wounds if allowed to pierce the fisherman's skin. Also noteworthy is their ability to give birth to live young, since most fish are hatched from fertilized eggs. Rockfish are commonly called rock cod and sea bass, but bear no close relationship to either the cod or bass families. At least ten varieties of the rockfish known to live in Puget Sound are commonly caught by sport anglers.

Although most rockfish are good eating, the favorite is the red variety, commonly known as red snapper. I often catch this fish in a ''hole,'' long identified by my expert fishermen neighbors, which is located just a few hundred yards offshore in front of my house. During the summer, it is nearly always possible to set out for dinner during a late afternoon slack tide, and an hour later return to shore with plenty of fish for the meal.

–Huachinago Puget Sound

I have prepared tasty red snapper in a number of different ways, but none is more appealing than this combination of fresh vegetables and fish fillets, inspired by a visit to Mexico several years ago.

½ lb. mushrooms, thinly sliced
1 large onion, cut into chunks
1 small zucchini, thinly sliced
4 tablespoons butter
1 garlic clove, mashed
2 lbs. red snapper fillets
2 large tomatoes, chopped
½ cup black olives, chopped
1 teaspoon oregano
½ teaspoon freshly ground black pepper
½ teaspoon salt

In medium frying pan, sauté mushrooms, onion, zucchini, and garlic in 2 tablespoons butter until tender. In large frying pan, pan-fry fillets in 2 tablespoons butter for 3 minutes on each side. Cover fish with tomatoes, cooked vegetables, and olives, and sprinkle with seasoning. Cover pan with tight-fitting lid and let steam over medium heat for 10 minutes or until fish flakes when touched with fork. Serves 4.

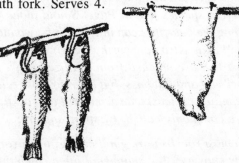

Cod

Both true and so-called cod are very common in Northwest waters, but they are not eaten here so much as they are in Scandinavia and New England. White-fleshed, with a firm texture and distinctive flavor, cod is excellent in fish stews or baked in a rich cream sauce. Ling cod is a particularly popular Northwest fish, as is sablefish (often called black cod).

–Baked Cod and Cheese Sauce

1½–2 lbs. cod fillets
2 tablespoons melted butter
1 garlic clove, mashed
½ cup grated sharp Cheddar cheese
¾ cup sour cream or crème fraîche
Chopped parsley

In long baking pan, place washed and dried fillets. Stir garlic into butter and pour over fish. Bake at 350° for 20 minutes or until fish flakes when touched with fork. Mix cheese and sour cream together and spread over fish. Return to oven and broil for 5 minutes or until sauce bubbles and turns brown. Garnish with chopped parsley. Serves 4.

—Baked Cod— with Vegetables

3 tablespoons olive oil
1 medium onion, finely chopped
2 garlic cloves, minced
¼ cup coriander or parsley, finely chopped
½ teaspoon salt
1 teaspoon fresh thyme
1 teaspoon fresh tarragon
2 cups fresh tomatoes, chopped
½ cup dry wine
1 lb. red potatoes, peeled and thinly sliced
¼ lb. grated fresh Parmesan cheese

In small saucepan heat oil and sauté onion and garlic. Add parsley, salt, and herbs and stir well. Then add tomatoes and wine and simmer over medium heat until liquid is reduced by a third. In buttered long baking pan, arrange fillets and potatoes and pour sauce over top. Cover pan with foil and bake at 375° for 20 minutes or until fish flakes when touched with fork. Remove foil, sprinkle with cheese, and place under broiler for 2 minutes until cheese melts. Serves 4.

—Puget Sound Fish Stew—

Fish stews are as unique and different as the kitchens where they origi-nate. The best fish and shellfish combinations are never the same twice. It is the special bounty of the day's effort that makes each fish stew a memorable feast.

The secret of delicious seafood stew is the consistent use of a savory stock that enhances, but doesn't dominate, the natural goodness of the fish. I think garlic is essential, used judiciously, and I also like to try different fresh herbs. Wine is always welcome in my homemade stock, as is olive oil—which adds a distinctive taste. Although I am still working on the per-fect stock, this formula is already a winner.

1 large onion, chopped
2 green peppers, chopped
2 cups canned tomatoes, chopped,
  ***or* 4 fresh tomatoes, peeled and chopped**

2 garlic cloves, minced
½ teaspoon salt
1 teaspoon dried tarragon
  or 1 tablespoon fresh
½ teaspoon chervil
1 Dungeness crab, cleaned
  and broken into pieces
12 mussels, washed and scrubbed
12 butter clams, washed and scrubbed
⅓ cup olive oil
1½ lbs. halibut, cut into 1½-inch pieces
1 cup dry white wine
¼ cup chopped parsley
2 lemons, cut into small wedges

Combine vegetables, garlic, salt, tarragon, and chervil, and toss to mix. In the bottom of large Dutch oven, layer crab, mussels, and clams. Pour in oil and add half of vegetable mix. Add fish and remainder of vegetables and pour wine over top. Bring to a boil, then cover and simmer for 15 to 20 minutes until mussels and clams open. Garnish with parsley and serve with hunks of fresh bread and lemon wedges. Serves 8.

–Cod Croquettes

Firmly textured fish, such as cod, makes excellent croquettes.

2 lbs. cod, cut into small pieces
4 tablespoons butter
2 tablespoons dry white wine
3 tablespoons flour
1¼ cups milk
1 tablespoon lemon juice
2 tablespoons chopped parsley
Bunch of scallions, finely chopped
Salt and pepper to taste
1 cup bread crumbs
2 eggs, beaten well
Oil for deep frying

In medium frying pan, cook fish in 1 tablespoon butter and wine for 10 minutes, turning fish frequently. Put remaining butter in top of double boiler, stir in flour, and cook for several minutes over medium heat, stirring constantly. Add milk and cook until thickened, beating well with wire whisk. Add fish to sauce and blend well. Then add lemon juice, parsley, and scallions, and simmer for 10 minutes, stirring occasionally. Add salt and pepper, remove from heat, and refrigerate overnight.

Form croquettes with fingers or two spoons and roll through bread crumbs, then eggs, then bread crumbs again. Drop into oil heated to 375° and deep fry until golden. Makes 12 croquettes. Serves 4.

–Seviche

Marinated raw fish, or seviche, is a wonderful change from a turn in the oven or the stockpot. The best marinades are spontaneous—inspired by your spice rack and refrigerator vegetable bin.

> **2 lbs. cod or sole fillets,**
>   **cut into long thin strips**
> **½ cup fresh lemon juice**
> **Dash Tabasco sauce**
> **¼ cup chopped parsley**
> **2 fresh tomatoes, finely chopped**
> **1 green pepper, finely chopped**
> **1 medium onion, finely chopped**
> **1 garlic clove, minced**
> **½ cup white wine vinegar**
> **½ teaspoon salt**
> **½ teaspoon sugar**
> **Lemon wedges**

Place fish in glass or ceramic bowl. Mix lemon juice, Tabasco, and parsley, and pour over fish. Refrigerate overnight. Combine tomatoes, pepper, onion, and garlic, and pour in vinegar blended with salt and sugar. Spoon vegetable mixture over fish and garnish with lemon wedges. Serves 6–8.

Smelt

The tiny silver smelt is another fish highly prized in the Pacific Northwest. Usually six inches long, smelt move in large schools through the inland waters of Washington and up the Columbia River. Several small communities in Puget Sound host smelt derbies in the late winter. The fish are caught by jigging, a method in which anything from a safety pin to a triple-barbed hook is tied to the end of a short line on a very light pole. The informality of jigging for smelt especially attracts the very young and the very old, for whom elaborate fishing tackle is simply a bother.

In the summer, smelt dipping is enjoyed on many different beaches throughout the sound, as the smelt schools change location. At high tide one can see fishermen standing shoulder to shoulder holding special nets to catch their prey. The nets are often three feet wide and can pick up several dozen smelt with one scoop.

These tiny creatures were known as candlefish to the Indians, who dried and burned them for their high oil content. Smelt are commonly eaten whole, after being dipped in milk and corn meal, then fried lightly in butter. Upwards of a dozen are usually consumed at one meal.

CHEESE AND COMPANY

It is said that since God gave Oregon one of the world's most spectacular seacoasts, Oregon happily gave the world delicious Tillamook cheese. Tillamook is a scenic coastal community, tucked peacefully between the mountains and the sea. Perhaps its beautiful setting inspired the original cheese makers, whose genius has been passed along through several generations.

Even the most nonchalant visitor to the Oregon coast will be unforgettably impressed by the over three hundred miles of breathtaking scenery. Towering headlands, unusual rock formations, sandy broad beaches, and giant dunes are only some of the more dramatic geographical features of this region. Over half of this natural treasure belongs to the citizens of the state in the form of carefully maintained public parks. Some are reserved for day use only, but many have well-planned camping facilities.

Every season of the year is inviting at the Oregon coast. There is always hiking, beachcombing, and simply gaping at mile after mile of majestic beauty. But my favorite season to visit is during the warm months of summer, when swimming is a popular activity.

The Coast Range between the Willamette Valley and the Pacific kept the pioneers away from the ocean's edge until 1851. Once discovered, this beautiful countryside attracted thousands of settlers, especially because of its mild climate and natural meadows, which made it a prime location for dairy farming. Herds of dairy cows produced heavily, but the farmers were unable to market large quantities of milk before it spoiled. Some of the local farmers therefore began to make butter and cheese. By 1900 cheese making was flourishing in Tillamook, which became the first town in America to market cheese under its own brand name.

Today nearly twenty million pounds of cheese are produced annually and sold in stores throughout the country. The Tillamook County Creamery Association, organized in 1909, operates a large factory in downtown Tillamook where visitors can see cheese being made. Milk is delivered daily to these "cheese kitchens" and is turned into medium (aged three to five months) and sharp (aged six to nine months) Cheddar-like cheese.

A brick of cheese is a natural for a picnic on the coast, as are some of the local seafood specialties. One of my favorite roadside stands near Tillamook offers smoked tuna and halibut, Dungeness crab from the ocean, and oysters from local bays. Combine any and all of that with a bottle or two of good wine and a loaf of homemade bread, and there is a marvelous lunch in store—on the beach, from a lookout, or up in the hills.

—Really Dark Rye

2 tablespoons baking yeast
1 cup warm water
2½ cups beer
⅓ cup margarine
1 cup molasses
1 tablespoon salt
1 tablespoon caraway seed
5 cups rye flour
4 cups whole-wheat flour
1 egg beaten with 1 tablespoon water

In large bowl dissolve yeast in water. Heat beer in medium saucepan until it starts to bubble. Remove from heat, add margarine, and stir until margarine melts. Add molasses, salt, and caraway seed. Cool and add to yeast. Beat in rye flour and add whole-wheat flour—a little at a time—until dough becomes too stiff to stir. Turn out on floured board and knead until smooth, adding flour as necessary to keep dough from sticking to board. Put dough in oiled bowl, lightly oil the top, and cover. Set in a warm place until double in bulk, about 1½ hrs. Punch down, turn out on lightly floured board, and cut in half. Shape into long ovals and place on greased baking sheet. Slash top of loaves and brush with egg. Let stand in warm place until double in bulk, about 1 hr. Bake at 350° for 40–45 minutes or until loaf sounds hollow when tapped.

Besides Tillamook, several other towns along the coast produce cheese. My favorite, from a small cooperative at Bandon, is a special product known as full-cream Cheddar. Produced from milk at the peak of its annual cream content, aged full-cream Cheddar is unfortunately in short supply.

Bandon is also the center of some thriving cranberry farms and hosts a festival to honor these grape-size beauties, which certainly deserve more attention in the kitchen than a routine appearance at Thanksgiving.

–Cranberry Bread

2 cups whole-wheat flour
1 cup brown sugar
½ teaspoon salt
1½ teaspoons baking powder
½ teaspoon soda
Juice and grated rind of 1 medium orange
2 tablespoons oil
1 egg
1 cup chopped walnuts
1 cup whole raw cranberries

Combine flour, brown sugar, salt, baking powder, and soda. Add grated orange rind. Mix juice from orange with oil and add enough boiling water to make ¾ cup liquid. Stir beaten egg into this liquid and add to flour mixture. Stir in nuts and fold in cranberries. Bake at 375° in greased loaf pan for 1 hour or until toothpick inserted into center comes out clean.

–Quick Cranberry Relish–

1 lb. fresh cranberries
1¼ cup sugar
Rind of 1 large orange, coarsely grated

Combine and refrigerate for 48 hours before use. Makes 2 pints.

GARDEN VEGETABLES

Once summer finally arrives in the Pacific Northwest, most backyard vegetable gardens produce heavily. The warmth and fertility of the soil, enhanced by the careful use of organic nutrients, as well as continually abundant moisture, make the successful growth of tasty vegetables easy for most Northwest gardeners.

In addition to favorable growing conditions, the Northwest is unusually free of the diseases and pests that plague gardens in other parts of the country. There are slugs, of course, which can devour an entire row of two-inch seedlings overnight and even an entire garden if they are ignored. I often reluctantly resort to the controlled use of highly toxic slug bait to eliminate them.

Peas

Assuming that the slugs are at bay, the first crop to appear in backyard gardens is usually peas. Most of the standard varieties do well in this climate, since peas like a cool growing season and are harvested in June and July before there is any real heat. No one I know ever plants enough garden peas or gets tired of eating them straight from the shell, lightly steamed, and topped with butter.

–Pork with Snow Peas

1½ lbs. fresh snow peas
½ cup soy sauce
½ cup sake or dry sherry
½ cup water
¼ cup sugar
6 garlic cloves, mashed
1 large piece of unpeeled ginger, scored
Freshly ground black pepper
4 thick loin pork chops

Snow peas are only available during the summer season. Picked for their delicate pods as well as the peas inside, snow peas are often used in stir-fry combinations. Pork is a natural with peas, and so is a meaty fish like halibut or sea bass.

Clean snow peas by removing stems, pulling fiber off edge, and rinsing in cold water. Soak in ice water for an hour if peas are not crisp.

In large frying pan combine soy, sake, water, sugar, garlic, and spices, and stir over low heat until sugar dissolves. Remove gingerroot and cook pork on each side for 3 minutes, then place in long baking pan. Pour sauce over top, cover pan with aluminum foil, and bake at 350° for 20 minutes.

Remove pork from oven and add peas to sauce, mixing well, and then smother pork with sauce and peas. Return to oven until peas are tender— about 10 minutes. Serve with steamed rice. Serves 4.
Note: If fish is substituted for pork, change the sauce by using ¼ cup soy sauce, 1 thinly sliced lemon, and 2 leeks, separated and sliced.

Lettuce

In most gardens, radishes are next to mature, but mine often get wormy and so the next real harvest is lettuce. I try to plant three or four different varieties and stagger the plantings two weeks apart, so that I can have fresh garden salads from mid-June through August. Both the red- and green-leaf varieties thrive on moderate summer temperatures. Romaine, too, never fails to produce spectacularly in my garden.

I tried limestone Bibb lettuce several years ago, after I had given up on several other varieties of head lettuce because they went to seed before becoming mature enough to harvest. The Bibb variety produces small, fairly compact heads with leaves that taste buttery and slightly sweet. I have learned to individually pick the mature leaves of both head and leaf lettuce, so that the remaining core can continue to sprout new leaves for several more weeks.

–Limestone
Lettuce Salad

Only very fresh lettuce should be used for this salad, and each leaf should be washed and dried with care. Homemade croutons, made from stale bread cut into cubes and soaked in melted garlic butter, are especially good.

24 lettuce leaves
Croutons
1 tablespoon white wine vinegar
1 tablespoon fresh lemon juice
4 tablespoons safflower oil
2 tablespoons olive oil
1 teaspoon Dijon mustard
Salt

Wash lettuce and sprinkle with croutons. Mix remaining ingredients, except salt, and drizzle over leaves. Add salt to taste. Serves 4.

Spinach

Spinach is another early crop in Northwest gardens. My experience has taught me that, of all vegetables, spinach must be watched very carefully, because just as soon as the weather gets warm, the plants will start to bolt and the leaves will quickly turn bitter and inedible. I sometimes get so frustrated with spinach that I plant Swiss chard instead, which tastes quite similar and is very easy to grow. But since spinach is essential to lots of things that I like to cook, at least one row usually gets planted each year.

–Baked Greens

This casserole is delicious made with spinach, beet greens, chard, or kale. It can be served as a main course, with the addition of ½ lb. of tofu (soybean curd) cubed and sprinkled on top.

2 lbs. spinach or other greens
½ cup water
1 teaspoon red wine vinegar
2 cups grated Swiss, Cheddar, or jack cheese

4 eggs
1 cup milk
½ teaspoon salt
1 teaspoon fresh oregano
1 teaspoon fresh basil

In Dutch oven steam greens in water and vinegar until leaves are just wilted and stalks are tender. Drain and arrange evenly in bottom of Dutch oven. Sprinkle with grated cheese. Beat eggs, milk, salt, and herbs together, and pour over greens and cheese. Bake at 375° for 30 minutes or until custard is set. Serves 4.

Potatoes

Getting children interested in the vegetable garden is a project that can't begin too soon. Potatoes make an enticing gardening project even for very young children, who can pick up the large pieces of seed potatoes and drop them into a row of waiting holes. The resulting plants are relatively quick to emerge from the soil, and, as soon as they flower, new potatoes can be harvested. Kids love to get into the act of harvesting potatoes, especially when four or six can be found in every shovelful.

Potatoes thrive west of the Cascades where they can be stored in the ground well into the fall, if the weather is dry. They are also grown in tremendous commercial quantities in the Columbia Basin of Washington and throughout eastern Oregon.

—New Potatoes in Dill Sauce

2 lbs. new potatoes
1 cup sour cream or yogurt
1 tablespoon lemon juice
1 teaspoon fresh dill weed
¼ cup chopped parsley
Salt and pepper to taste

Scrub unpeeled potatoes and cut in half. Steam in Dutch oven until tender. Stir together sour cream, lemon juice, and dill. Pour over cooked potatoes and garnish with parsley. Serve hot or cold. Serves 4.

—Basque Potatoes

There are two large Basque communities in this part of the country, one centered in the sheep country of Idaho and the other around San Francisco. One Saturday afternoon, a friend of mine, then a child of ten, was taken by her uncle to eat at a Basque restaurant where the chefs had finished cooking for their guests and were busy making lunch for themselves. My friend and her uncle were welcomed and presented with plates piled high with ethnic specialties, including these wonderful herbed potatoes.

8 medium white potatoes
4 tablespoons butter
2 tablespoons olive oil
2 cloves garlic, mashed
1 teaspoon paprika
Dash cayenne
1 teaspoon dried rosemary
1 teaspoon fresh thyme
¼ cup chopped parsley

Scrub potatoes and cut in half if large, but leave whole if medium to small. Melt butter in large frying pan over low heat and add oil. Add garlic, paprika, and cayenne, and stir. Crush rosemary using mortar and pestle, until well ground. Add rosemary and thyme to butter, and sprinkle in parsley. Stir entire mixture well. Roll potatoes in mixture until well coated. Bake in same pan at 375° for 20 minutes or until potatoes are golden and tender, basting occasionally. Serves 4–6.

Carrots

The carrot season seems to be one of the longest in my garden, counting the thinning of baby carrots (which can and should be used in the kitchen) all the way through to the last mature row, which I pull up and store in a makeshift root cellar. The number of different varieties of carrots astonishes me. I try to plant at least three every year—one old favorite, a new one recommended by another gardener, and a third that no one seems to have tried before.

–Carrots and Mint–––––––––

1 lb. fresh young carrots, peeled
4 tablespoons butter
4 leaves fresh mint, chopped
¼ teaspoon cinnamon
Salt and pepper to taste

In large saucepan steam carrots whole. Cream butter with mint. Drain carrots and slather with butter, then sprinkle lightly with cinnamon. Add salt and pepper to taste. Serve hot. Makes 3–4 servings.

–Carrot Compote–––––––––

This simple marinade for fresh carrots creates a tasty condiment for serving with wild birds or game.

2 cups coarsely grated carrots
2 cups orange juice
½ cup currants

Combine ingredients and chill overnight. Serves 4.

–Island Carrot Cake–––––––

When I was first learning to cook from something other than a package, one of my first successes was carrot bread, made from a recipe I found in a discarded notebook in the basement of the house where I lived. I still make this bread occasionally, partly because it tastes good, but also to remind myself of when and where my interest in cooking with seasonal abundance first began.

3 eggs
1½ cups oil
2 cups brown sugar
2 cups grated carrot
1 cup crushed pineapple
3 cups all-purpose flour
1 teaspoon soda
1 teaspoon salt
3 teaspoons vanilla
3 teaspoons cinnamon

Beat together eggs, oil, and sugar. Stir in carrot and pineapple, then add flour, soda, and salt, and stir until batter is smooth. Add vanilla and cinnamon, stirring well. Bake in 2 greased bread pans at 325° for 1 hour. Serve warm or cold. Makes 25 slices.

Note: For variety, 1 cup chopped walnuts, sunflower seeds, or plumped raisins can be added to the batter.

Zucchini

Ten years ago, when someone mentioned zucchini, most people thought it was a classy Italian sports car or an unusual kind of pasta. That has changed in the past few years, and now nearly everyone not only knows this flavorful squash, but has a favorite method or two of putting it on the table.

As a gardener, it's easy to get too enthusiastic about zucchini, to the point where common sense gets left behind. I am one of those who tries to be cautious about this vegetable, but invariably end up with twice as much as I can possibly cook, preserve, or give away. It sometimes seems that the fewer plants I set out, the more squash I grow.

Local contests spring up in the Northwest, as elsewhere I am sure, to creatively dispose of—excuse me, prepare—zucchini in yet another cleverly disguised way. Events like these have spawned such culinary triumphs as zucchini chocolate cake and a lot of excellent relishes, pickles, soups, and main dishes.

–Zucchini Lasagne

Zucchini is often used as a meat replacement by creative vegetarian cooks, partly because of its meaty texture, but also because of its distinctive flavor. This lasagne is one such delicious recipe.

¾ lb. lasagne noodles
4 cups raw grated zucchini
2 cups grated mozzarella or jack cheese

–Sauce

1 medium onion, chopped
3 cloves garlic, minced
3 tablespoons olive oil
½ teaspoon oregano
1 teaspoon dried basil
4 cups whole tomatoes, drained
1 small can tomato paste
2 tablespoons brown sugar
½ cup parsley, finely chopped
1 lb. mushrooms, sliced

–Filling

1 teaspoon coriander seed
½ teaspoon anise seed
½ cup cottage cheese
1 cup ricotta cheese
½ cup yogurt

Sauté onion and garlic in oil in Dutch oven until tender. Add oregano, basil, tomatoes, tomato paste, sugar, parsley, and mushrooms. Simmer for 20 minutes, stirring occasionally. Then turn off heat and set sauce aside.

Finely grind coriander and anise seeds with mortar and pestle. Add to cottage cheese, ricotta, and yogurt, and beat well. Cook lasagne noodles in boiling salted water according to package directions until soft, and drain. In greased long baking pan layer a third of the noodles, then zucchini, pour on half of sauce, then add another third of the noodles, top with cheese mixture, add remainder of noodles, and cover with rest of sauce. Top with grated cheese and bake for 35–45 minutes at 375°. Sprinkle with freshly grated Parmesan cheese just before serving. Serves 6.

–Zucchini Patties

Here is another main dish with zucchini. Try the patty mixture cooked and served in hot tortillas.

3 cups grated zucchini
1 small onion, chopped
1 large egg
½ cup bread crumbs
½ teaspoon garlic powder
½ teaspoon cumin
Salt and pepper to taste
Oil for frying
Grated fontina, jack, or Parmesan cheese

Combine first seven ingredients and drop by spoonfuls into hot oil. Fry lightly on one side until brown, turn and fry on other side. Sprinkle with grated cheese while second side is browning. Serves 4.

–Lentil-Zucchini Soup–

The lentils give this soup substance; the soy, onion, and garlic lend interest. Other vegetables—especially broccoli, cauliflower, or green beans—can be used.

12 finger-size zucchini
2 cups lentils
3 cloves garlic, mashed
1 medium onion, sliced
2 tablespoons olive oil
3 stalks celery
3 carrots, sliced
¼ cup parsley, chopped
1 small can tomato paste
3 tablespoons soy sauce
1 tablespoon summer savory
Few sprigs fresh basil
Few sprigs fresh thyme
Salt and pepper to taste

Remove ends from zucchini, slice lengthwise, and set aside. Cover lentils with approximately 4 cups water in Dutch oven and bring to boil. Cover and simmer until tender. Sauté garlic and onion in oil in medium frying pan and then add to lentils. Add tomato paste and soy sauce, and stir. Combine herbs, salt and pepper, and vegetables, and simmer until vegetables are tender. Serves 6.

–Zucchini Soup

This very simple zucchini soup can be served either warm or ice cold. The corn at the bottom of the bowl is a welcome surprise, and lots of freshly ground black pepper floating on the top is essential.

> **3 medium zucchini (6 to 8 inches long)**
> **2 cups light cream**
> **1 teaspoon salt**
> **2–6 drops Tabasco sauce**
> **1 ear of corn**
> **Freshly cracked black pepper**

Wash zucchini, cut into large chunks, and steam in large saucepan until soft. Purée in blender and add cream, salt, and Tabasco to taste. Steam corn for 10 minutes or until kernels easily come away from cob. Add kernels to soup and serve with pepper to taste. Serves 4.

Corn

Corn needs a lot of sunshine, of course, so that most Pacific Northwest gardens west of the Cascades don't produce corn until late August. East of the mountains, however, corn thrives in the hot and sunny Yakima Valley and is brought to Seattle by the truckload much earlier in the summer. But as good as this Yakima corn can be, there is nothing quite like corn grown in your own garden.

The secret, of course, is to pick, steam, and serve the ears in as short a time as possible. The minute the corn is removed from its stalk, its high sugar content begins to turn to starch—so the less time that elapses between the garden and the dinner table, the sweeter the corn will be. I have friends who put a pot of water on the stove to boil, head to the garden, gather a few ears of corn, and then sprint back to the kitchen as quickly as possible. Some people even boast of actually shucking the ear while still on the stalk, thereby eliminating precious minutes wasted in the kitchen.

–Corn Relish

Although the best way to enjoy corn is simply steamed on the cob, slathered in butter, and lightly salted, there is a particular corn relish that is well worth making, especially with those last few ears at the end of the season that have probably become starchy anyway.

2 cups cider vinegar
½ lb. brown sugar
2 tablespoons celery seed
1 tablespoon dry mustard
2 tablespoons salt
5 cups fresh corn kernels
 (approximately 10 ears)
2 cups onions, chopped
½ cup green sweet pepper, chopped
¼ cup red sweet pepper, chopped

Combine cider vinegar and sugar in Dutch oven and stir over medium heat until sugar dissolves. Add celery seed, mustard, and salt, and bring to a boil. Add vegetables, partially cover, and simmer for 15 minutes. Makes 4 pints.

–Corn Chowder

Most people think chowder means clams. Few would think of substituting corn for clams. This hearty recipe makes exceptional eating.

4 tablespoons butter
1 medium onion, finely chopped
3 stalks celery, chopped
3 medium potatoes, diced with skins intact
2 cups water
Bay leaf
½ teaspoon salt
Freshly ground black pepper
2 cups whole canned tomatoes, chopped
3–4 large ears of corn
3 tablespoons flour
½ cup milk
1 cup cream
½ cup parsley, chopped

Sauté onion and celery in large saucepan in butter until wilted but not brown. Add potatoes, water, bay leaf, and seasonings, and simmer until potatoes are tender. Add tomatoes and kernels cut from ears of corn. Heat flour and milk in small saucepan until boiling. Add to soup, stirring constantly. Taste and correct seasoning. Add cream and simmer 15 minutes. Garnish with parsley.

Dips

I used to think dips were strictly for serving at cocktail parties, either with or without vegetables. Not so, I have learned, especially when there is a backyard garden bursting with inspiration for the cook. These dips can be the center of a lunchtime potpourri of raw vegetables, or a good afternoon snack for kids. Vegetables usually eaten cooked—such as turnips, kohlrabi, cauliflower, and green beans—seem especially crisp and flavorful when served with dips.

–Curry Dip

1 cup yogurt
¼ cup mayonnaise
2 teaspoons curry powder
2 tablespoons honey
Dash paprika

Beat ingredients well. Makes 1 cup.

–Cucumber Dip

½ large cucumber or 2 lemon cucumbers
1 clove garlic, mashed
1 teaspoon dill weed
2 tablespoons lemon juice
½ cup yogurt
4 oz. cream cheese
Chives, finely chopped

Scrub cucumbers, chop coarsely, and combine in blender with garlic. Whirl mixture until pulverized. Add remaining ingredients, except chives, and blend until smooth. Chill and garnish with chopped chives. Makes 1 cup.

—Hummus———————————

Hummus is a Middle Eastern classic, usually spread on the pocket bread called pita and eaten as a tasty nourishing meal. Although a bit spicy for some palates, it makes a terrific vegetable dip. Extra lemon juice may be added to obtain a thinner consistency.

> **1 cup cooked garbanzo beans (chick peas)**
> **½ cup sesame seeds**
> **4 cloves garlic, mashed**
> **4 tablespoons lemon juice, freshly squeezed**
> **4 tablespoons safflower oil**
> **1 teaspoon coriander seeds, crushed**
> **½ teaspoon salt**
> **½ teaspoon cumin**
> **¼ cup chopped parsley**

Purée ingredients in blender until smooth. Makes about 2 cups.

—Vegetable Marinade———

I often collect a few pieces of a dozen different vegetables, wash them well, toss them into a crock or large jar, and fill it to the top with a simple marinade. Variety is essential; I find that green beans, scallions, broccoli, Brussels sprouts, and carrots, for example, make a good combination. The result is somewhere along the road to a genuine pickle, but still reminiscent of the day when the vegetables were first brought into the kitchen.

> **1 cup tarragon vinegar**
> **2 tablespoons celery seed**
> **1 tablespoon salt**
> **½ cup water**
> **1 teaspoon dry mustard**
> **Dash Tabasco sauce**

Combine, mix well, and pour over raw vegetables. Let mixture stand to combine flavors for at least two or three days before serving. Makes 1½ cups, sufficient to marinate about 4 cups of vegetables.

—Vegetable Stew—

A vegetable stew provides a marvelous opportunity for both the beginning cook and the sophisticated expert to show off. The main ingredients in this version come almost entirely from my August garden harvest. The exception is eggplant, which needs more warmth and sun to mature than it can possibly get in a Northwest garden, and so must be grown here in greenhouses.

1 large onion, sliced
3 garlic cloves, minced
5 tablespoons olive oil
2 cups zucchini, cut in 1-inch chunks
1 cup carrot, thinly sliced
½ cup celery with leaves, sliced
1 medium turnip, cut in 1-inch chunks
1 cup green beans, cut into 2-inch pieces
1 cup red cabbage, chopped
1 small eggplant, cut in 1-inch chunks
4 cups whole tomatoes with juice
½ cup red wine
¾ cup chopped parsley
3 bay leaves
1 teaspoon fresh thyme
1 teaspoon oregano
1 teaspoon summer savory
Salt and pepper to taste
Sour cream
Few sprigs of parsley

Sauté onion and garlic in oil in large Dutch oven or stockpot. Add vegetables and wine and bring to a boil, then let simmer until vegetables are almost tender. Add herbs, salt and pepper, and simmer gently for 10 more minutes. Garnish with fresh parsley and a dollop of sour cream. Serves 6.

Stir-frying

One of the first invitations to dinner that I received after arriving in the Northwest featured a delicious combination of shellfish and vegetables, lightly steamed, brilliant in color, and surprisingly crisp in texture. Such perfection seemed very complicated to me at the time. My host then explained the stir-fry method of cooking. All that is necessary is a wok, a sharp slicing knife or cleaver, and a variety of very fresh ingredients. Since I had never seen such bright, firm vegetables that had been cooked or such perfectly steamed fish, I became an immediate convert to this classic method of Chinese cooking.

Subsequent experience has taught me that, although an ordinary heavy metal frying pan with a tight-fitting lid will suffice, a wok, the concave Chinese stainless-steel or aluminum cooking pan, is certainly helpful in cooking with this method. To stir-fry means to cook slices of meat, seafood, or vegetables in oil, stirring them rapidly to ensure even heating. If necessary, they may then be covered tightly and allowed to steam in their own juices. Not only is this method of preparation quick and easy, but the results are both aesthetically appealing and healthful. The color of the food, especially of vegetables, is retained and even enhanced, and most nutrients remain intact.

When stir-frying vegetables, those that require the longest cooking time should be placed on the bottom of the pan. If several different vegetables are used, they should be layered so that those that just need a few minutes of heat are on top. For example, in the following recipe broccoli would be at the bottom of the wok and spinach at the top.

–Stir-Fried Vegetables–

¼ cup peanut oil
1 1-inch piece of ginger, chopped
1 clove garlic, mashed
Dash cayenne
1 cup carrots, sliced
1 cup onion, sliced
1 cup golden beets, sliced
2 cups broccoli, sliced
1 cup bok choy, chopped
1 pound spinach, coarsely chopped
¼ cup soy sauce

Heat oil in wok with gingerroot, garlic, and cayenne. Remove ginger and garlic. Add vegetables and stir to coat with oil. Sprinkle with soy sauce and cover tightly. Steam over medium high heat until vegetables are tender but crisp. Serves 4.

—Vegetable Tempura—

Tempura is the Japanese name for fish, meat, or vegetables fried in a light egg batter. In this recipe, the beer gives the batter a light, almost flaky quality when fried. To test the temperature of the cooking oil, toss a bread cube into the center of the pan after heating the oil for several minutes. When the bread browns in about a minute, the oil is sufficiently hot.

1⅓ cups flour
1 teaspoon salt
1 tablespoon vegetable oil
2 eggs, slightly beaten
½ cup flat beer
Oil for deep-frying

Mix together flour, salt, vegetable oil, and eggs. Add beer gradually and stir well. Allow the batter to set for several hours in refrigerator

Try any of these vegetables, sliced and patted dry:
Table-tag

Green beans	**Zucchini**	**Onions**
Sweet potatoes	**Winter squash**	**Broccoli**
Green peppers	**Cauliflower**	**Asparagus**
	Beets	

In wok or large frying pan heat enough oil to cover vegetables. When oil reaches 375°, dip vegetables in batter and fry until golden. Remove with slotted spoon and drain briefly on paper before serving.

FALL

GRAPES AND WINE

Bunches of green and purple grapes glisten in the sunshine of a warm October day, hanging in great clusters from the sturdy leafy vines. The wine maker has finally given the signal—at last, the grapes are ready—and so the annual crush begins. The novice picker finds harvesting almost hypnotic and eats nearly as many grapes as he or she tosses into waiting boxes during the first few minutes. But the syrupy sweetness of the ripe wine grapes finally begins to cloy, so the boxes fill quickly as the harvest continues far into the afternoon.

Of all the fall harvests, none seems to bring so much immediate pleasure and eager expectation as the gathering of grapes in wine-producing regions throughout the world. In America such purposeful activity often brings together an assortment of families, neighbors, and friends at the smaller wineries that flourish in California and the Pacific Northwest. Oregon and Washington wine making is an infant industry by California standards, but it is growing steadily in size, reputation, and the production of fine wine.

For decades the Northwest was considered too extreme in temperature east of the Cascades and too rainy to the west to successfully grow the great wine grapes of France and Germany that thrive in the Napa and Sonoma valleys of California. Yet vinifera vines were grown near Portland at the turn of the century and produced prizewinning wine. Vineyards were also established on several islands in southern Puget Sound by some of the original settlers in the 1870s.

Last fall, vintners David and Diana Lett invited me and several friends to pick grapes at the Eyrie Vineyards, some thirty miles southwest of Portland and near the town of Dundee. Our task on that particular day was to harvest the brilliant purple Gewurtztraminer variety, as well as the sensationally fragrant Muscats. We filled a stack of large boxes, which would be taken the next day by Lett to his winery seven miles from the vineyards at McMinnville.

Our enthusiasm remained unbounded as we harvested on into the afternoon. In keeping with the celebratory spirit of the day, Lett brought out several bottles of earlier vintages from these same vines and opened them for us to enjoy while we worked.

The harvest that day ended long before sunset, and a discussion of dinner ensued. The Letts are quite experienced in feeding the crowds of willing workers who show up to help with harvest. At their suggestion, a salmon had been purchased, which was to be poached in court bouillon and served with several different sauces. The fish was a great success with everyone—even the children, whose cheeks looked permanently stained with juice from the ripened grapes.

To accompany the salmon, the Letts opened bottles of Pinot gris, a light, fruity, but very dry wine. American winemakers have virtually ignored the Pinot gris grape, which is a major variety in the Alsace region of France, where it is made into the popular Tokay D'Alsace. Eyrie is the only vineyard in this country currently producing this delightful Pinot gris and their bottling is very small.

Winemaker Lett arrived in the Willamette Valley in 1966 to plant grapes and produce great wines. A graduate of the esteemed viticulture program at the University of California at Davis, he was looking for a place to grow Pinot noir, the grapes that produce the wines of Burgundy. Pinot noir grapes need a cooler, wetter climate than is generally present in California, so Lett considered various locations throughout the world.

After several years of searching for the ideal place to plant his vineyard, Lett settled on the Red Hills of Dundee in the Willamette Valley. For a prospective wine maker, this area was as untried as the Napa Valley had been a hundred years before. Local farmers scoffed at his efforts and assured him that grapes would never grow well enough in the valley to produce good wine.

Lett disproved local skeptics with his first bottling in 1970, and he has cultivated an enthusiastic following ever since. The Letts were the first vintners in the Willamette Valley, and now there are eight other wineries. Although certain grapes are growing better than others, there is still much experimentation with new varieties. Excitement runs high for the undiscovered possibilities of the wines of the Willamette. Although several wine makers have carved a niche in the regional market, as well as in the expanding national one, David and Diana Lett are particularly recognized for their initiative, ability, and results.

APPLES AND SWEET CIDER

Although fall harvest means grapes to some and pumpkins to others in the Pacific Northwest, apples are Washington for most of the rest of America. Over 30 percent of the nation's table apples are grown in the central valleys of Washington. The center of operations for the commercial apple growers is Wenatchee, a town northeast of Seattle on the eastern side of the Cascades. Thousands of acres of apple orchards surround Wenatchee and continue down the Columbia River toward Yakima. These orchards are so heavily planted that the blossoms scent the entire valley for several weeks in the spring.

An annual apple festival is held in the late spring, and the harvest usually begins in September. Many a Northwest teenager has worked a season or two of apple picking, side by side with thousands of Mexican migrants brought in to pick the crop. As is often the case with regional specialties, the most perfect apples are shipped to faraway markets by the trainload, where they are guaranteed to bring premium prices.

For those who live west of the Cascades, apples are also plentiful in well-tended backyard orchards as well as on trees untended for years. Apple trees are remarkably hardy and will continue to bear for as long as twenty years even without care. These apples may not be prizewinners in appearance, but they are nonetheless excellent for cooking and cider making.

Although some twenty different varieties grow successfully on the wet side of the mountains, the apple that many people prefer is the Gravenstein. A deliciously sweet eating apple, the Gravenstein is also tart enough to use for cooking. But perhaps best of all, a bin of Gravensteins is perfect for making gallons of freshly pressed apple cider, which is a favorite weekend project among Puget Sound friends and neighbors during October and even into November.

A typical day with the apple press begins early with a trip to local taverns, restaurants, and markets to collect emply gallon jugs. Once the jars have been rounded up, they are thoroughly scrubbed and set outside to dry. Then the press is made ready for a day of very hard work. My press has seen at least fifty seasons of cider making and usually needs a little encouragement with aerosol lubricant to turn and squeeze once again.

Once cleaned and ready for use, the press is moved out to the orchard. Nearly a dozen trees, some more prolific than others, stand ready for harvest. There are several different types, many of which are unidentified, but the apples we rely most upon grow on four large Gravenstein trees.

The press is awkward and cumbersome to move. It stands nearly three feet high but must be elevated another couple of feet in order to be operated comfortably. All of the wooden parts are well aged and rather indestructible oak; the machine parts are cast iron and sturdy. This press was built to last for generations, thankfully, but as a result it is awfully difficult to operate unless one's arm and shoulder muscles are well tuned. It is always necessary to recruit at least half a dozen workers in order to keep the press running continually for an afternoon, during which time up to fifty gallons of cider can be made.

The apples are now gathered, if they haven't been picked earlier in the week. Everyone from small child to elderly grandmother helps out with this task, since the windfalls are as valuable as the fruit that is still hanging on the tree. Since anyone can pick up fallen apples, almost everyone seems willing to join in this part of the day's activity.

The fruit that is still on the trees is sometimes harvested with a special long-handled picker. More often, though, a ''shaker'' climbs part way into the branches and shakes them heartily. The apple rain lasts for a few seconds, and then it is an easy job to fill several empty bins. There is no need to worry about bruising the fruit as it is gathered. The press will turn it all into sweet cider, as long as the fruit is not rotten.

Once the crank is turning in a steady rhythm, the apples are thrown into the chipper several at a time. The rotation of the chipper chops the apples into small pieces, automatically releasing a lot of juice even before the pieces are placed under the press. Once the chipped apples are put under the press plate, the lid is tightened and the cider then begins to flow in a steady stream. The neck of the waiting container is covered with cheesecloth, which strains any pulp from the liquid.

Each hand at the press is entitled to several gallons of the results of the day's hard work. I drink as much of my share while it is still fresh as I

can, and I put some away to turn into the year's supply of vinegar. I also like to use the fresh cider to baste almost any fowl or pork dish, so I usually freeze two or three gallons to use as basting liquid throughout the year. Plastic containers are best for freezing cider. Several inches of air space should be left at the top of each container after filling, to allow for the expansion of the freezing liquid.

Unless it is pasteurized within a few days of pressing, apple cider will quickly turn to vinegar. Pasteurizing the cider is a simple matter of boiling it for ten minutes, which kills the wild yeast contained in it and enables the cider to remain sweet. Pasteurized cider should be kept under refrigeration.

–Glazed Pork Loin

This glazed pork loin combines savory herbs with the distinctive sweetness of jellied cranberry sauce and repeated basting with apple cider.

2 cloves garlic, mashed
1 teaspoon sage
½ teaspoon nutmeg
1 teaspoon dry mustard
2 teaspoons salt
½ teaspoon pepper
4-lb. pork loin
2 onions, sliced
1 cup apple cider
¼ cup jellied cranberry sauce

Mix garlic with sage, nutmeg, mustard, salt, and pepper. Rub resulting paste well into meat. Spread sliced onions in center of a long baking pan and place meat, fat side up, on top. Pour cider over meat and roast at 325° for 1 hour. Baste frequently with pan juices.

Remove roast from oven and slash fat several times. Spoon cranberry sauce into cuts and return to oven for 1 hour. Serves 6.

–Roast Pheasant–
Baked in
Apple Cider

Apple cider is a particularly tasty baste for wild fowl, such as mallard, widgeon, or pheasant, and it is also delicious with chicken. The stuffing can be varied to include water chestnuts, walnuts, or oysters.

2–4 lb. pheasant, plucked and cleaned
4 tablespoons butter
1 cup whole-wheat bread cubes
1 teaspoon sage
Salt and pepper
1 small onion, finely chopped
1 small apple, finely chopped
1 egg, lightly beaten
3–4 strips uncooked bacon
1 cup apple cider

Salt cavity of bird well. Melt butter in medium frying pan and lightly fry bread cubes, adding sage and salt and pepper to taste. Mix onion and apples into bread mixture and add egg, blending thoroughly. Stuff cavity of bird. Using toothpicks, pin bacon strips over breast and place on a rack in long baking pan. Bake at 350° for 45 minutes or until done, basting frequently with pan juices and apple cider. Serves 2–3.

–Dutch Cabbage–

One good reason, I imagine, that cabbage and apples go so well together may be that they are both harvested at about the same time. Although the early cabbage varieties can be picked as soon as late July in the Pacific Northwest, I prefer to plant mine rather late and bring it into the kitchen along with the pumpkins and Brussels sprouts.

A friend of mine from Amsterdam was raised on cabbage and rates this combination very highly.

2 lbs. red or green cabbage,
  coarsely shredded
4 large apples, peeled and thinly sliced
1 cup uncooked rice
½ cup brown sugar
1 teaspoon salt
5 cups water
1 cup apple cider vinegar

In Dutch oven place layer of cabbage, then apples, then sprinkle ⅓ of rice, ⅓ of sugar, and ⅓ of salt over top. Repeat twice. Pour water and vinegar over all and bake at 300° for 3 hours or until rice is completely cooked. Serves 4.

—Brandy Cider Punch—

Cider kept sweet by freezing or pasteurizing makes an excellent punch. I served hot spiced cider with brandy at my wedding and it proved to be more popular with the guests than the champagne!

1 gallon apple cider
6 whole cloves
4 cinnamon sticks
6 whole cardamom, shelled
½ teaspoon nutmeg, freshly grated
Fifth of brandy
3 oranges, cut into thin slices
2 lemons, cut into thin slices

Simmer cider and spices over medium heat in Dutch oven for 15 minutes. Remove from heat and add brandy. Garnish with fruit and serve immediately. Makes 16 servings.

APPLE WINE AND SPARKLING CIDER

I know few ways of experiencing more pleasure from the seasonal abundance of the Pacific Northwest than drinking a bottle of homemade sparkling apple cider. Even serious wine connoisseurs are impressed by the quality of this beverage, which is a delicious accompaniment to almost any

meat dish and is also wonderful when served as an aperitif. For those who take the time to make this champagne, there is great reward for relatively little effort. Sparkling apple champagne is the embodiment of a successful harvest, reminding us of fall, regardless of when we fill our glasses.

I am no fan of the usual garden-variety homemade fruit wines. Sparkling cider, however, is different. In Canada it is bottled and sold commercially on liquor-store shelves next to beer. B.C. cider, as it is known in Seattle, is also available in pubs and restaurants throughout western Canada and would no doubt have a lively market in America if it were available.

At the moment, though, we must be content to make cider at home, which takes from nine to twelve months from beginning to end. A minimum of equipment, a few powders and tablets, and a lot of fresh cider and sugar is all that is necessary. To become familiar with the procedure, it is best to make only five gallons the first time. Larger quantities can easily be made once the technique is mastered.

To make five gallons of apple wine, which is the first step toward apple champagne, a bit of reusable hardware is required (prices approximate):

2 5-gallon carboys	**($5 each)**
2 airlocks	**($1 each)**
Sacchrometer	**($3)**
Siphon hose	**($2)**

All of these supplies can be purchased at a wine-making equipment shop. The following recipe originated at Aetna Wine Supply in Seattle, where Joe Combs and his family have been in the business for fifty years. They are more than willing to answer questions and otherwise assist the beginning wine maker, and thus have helped me time and time again.

—Apple Wine

5 gallons fresh apple cider
5 Campden tablets (sodium bisulphite)
1¼ teaspoons yeast nutrient
1¼ teaspoons pectic enzyme powder
5–7 lbs. sugar
5 grams Montrachet wine yeast
5 rounded teaspoons sparkolloid

Each of the cider additives has a specific purpose in the wine-making process. The yeast nutrient *contains the necessary nitrogen nourishment to promote the proper growth of the wine yeast.* Pectic enzyme *is a clarifier that aids the cider in settling and speeds the normal clarification process.* Campden tablets *kill wild yeast and other unwanted organisms.* Wine yeast *creates proper fermentation and turns the sugar into alcohol.* Sparkolloid *is a seaweed derivative that also helps clarification.*

Step 1: Add the Campden tablets, yeast nutrient, pectic enzyme, and sugar to cider in a carboy. The amount of sugar to be added is determined by the reading on the sacchrometer. To take a measurement with a sacchrometer, pour a sample from the carboy into tall jar or glass. When the instrument reads 24 on the Brix scale, the sugar content is sufficient. Before a sample is taken, sugar should be added directly to the carboy and shaken for even distribution. For five gallons of cider, the amount of sugar needed will be between five and seven pounds, depending on how naturally sweet the cider was to begin with.
Let the cider mixture set for 24 to 72 hours.

Step 2: Add the wine yeast according to package directions and place the carboy in a location where temperature is 70°. Use an airlock to close the carboy during fermentation, filling it partially with water, to allow the escape of carbon dioxide from the fermenting wine. When the sacchrometer reads 4 or less (4 is recommended for sweet wine, 2 for dry), fermentation has virtually ceased. This usually takes 6 to 12 weeks, depending on the location of the carboy and the rate at which the yeast is working.

Step 3: Siphon the finished wine into a clean carboy and clarify with sparkolloid, prepared according to the package directions. Let it settle until clear (usually 3 to 4 weeks), preferably storing in a 60° place.

Step 4:   When wine is clear, siphon into a clean carboy and reserve 2 quarts of apple wine.

–Sparkling Cider————

To make sparkling cider from apple wine, you will need some more equipment (prices approximate):

> **20 champagne bottles   ($6)**
> **20 plastic corks   ($1)**
> **20 wire hoods   ($1)**
> **1 package champagne yeast   ($.75)**

You will also need the reserved five gallons of apple wine and 1½ pounds of sugar.

Step 1:   Begin with 4½ gallons of wine in the carboy and 2 quarts in a separate container. Add 1 quart of water to the reserved wine and ½ pound of sugar, and bring to a boil. Let cool to room temperature and pour 1 pint of wine mixture into a quart bottle and remainder into a gallon bottle.

Step 2:   Start the champagne yeast in a cup, fermenting according to package directions. When actively fermenting, add half the wine from quart bottle. When the yeast and wine start fermenting, add to the remainder of wine in quart bottle. When this wine becomes active, add to the wine in the gallon bottle.

Step 3:   While waiting for the gallon bottle to show signs of fermentation, add 1 pound of sugar to the wine in the carboy. Add the contents of the gallon bottle to the carboy as soon as activity is noticed.

Step 4:   When the carboy shows signs of fermentation, transfer the contents to the champagne bottles and cork and wire them. Store the bottles in a cool place—upside down on their corks.
Note: The reasons for this seemingly tedious process of adding the fermenting wine in small increments to the carboy are: 1) if the champagne yeast were added directly to the carboy, the wine would probably never clarify, and 2) there would be a permanently yeastly taste to the finished product because the yeast could not complete its work before being killed by the alcohol.

Step 5:   The bottles should be rotated daily for 3 to 4 months, about a quarter turn each day. When all the sediment appears to be lodged on the cork (you can see it moving slowly down the neck), undo the wire hood and remove the cork, immediately placing thumb over neck opening.

Step 6:   Right the uncorked bottle and top off with apple wine. Recork and store it in a cool place. Cider will be ready to drink in 8 months, but it is best when held for up to 2 years.

APPLES FOR EATING

The history books tell us that apples first arrived in Washington in 1827, via a Hudson's Bay Company schooner that had traveled around Cape Horn. The first apple seeds were planted at the Hudson's Bay trading post at Fort Vancouver, near the mouth of the Columbia River. Those seeds produced a tree which is still thriving and bearing fruit nearly a century and a half later.

From such modest beginnings the apple industry developed in the irrigated valleys of central Washington, where fruit trees grow well in the mineral-rich soil and relatively temperate climate. Many different varieties were tried for commercial production, but only six survived the competition successfully enough to meet the market demand. Of those, Red Delicious and Golden Delicious account for nearly 85 percent of the current total crop.

Not surprisingly—since it is the single most popular eating apple in America—Red Delicious alone are grown on almost half of all the commercial trees in Washington. This variety is recommended only for eating out of hand, but its golden cousin can also be used in cooking. (Interestingly, the flesh of the Golden Delicious remains white longer after being cut than does that of any other apple.)

Due to their tart flesh and good keeping qualities, Winesaps are considered the best all-purpose apple. Jonathans offer many of the Winesap characteristics but are extra juicy. The pale green Newtown, notably very firm, is also quite tart and is my favorite cooking apple. Each of the major Washington varieties is just fine for eating out of hand, except perhaps the thick-skinned Rome Beauty, an apple that is really best for cooking.

Modern "controlled atmosphere" methods of storage greatly retard the natural aging of fruit. Apples are now available at groceries from fall harvest through the following summer, and fresh Red Delicious and Golden Delicious can be purchased for nearly ten months of the year.

Apple Pie

A marvelous modification of the Great American Favorite, the following apple cream pie is tasty when cool, but is best served hot with an optional slice of good Cheddar. It was presented in the latter way one evening to a party of six, one of whom went home to compose this lyrical tribute:

A Rambling Line to Mrs. Anderson's Sour Cream Apple Pie

Never had love been as sudden,
post-industrially instantaneous,
computerspit
man on the moon
(whatever happened to romance?).

We'd only just met,
already
I knew I couldn't live without her.
Television montage,
horizontal hold on me
(in a neighbor's living room)
Tuesday prime time.
Lips sweet,
milk and honey
(this must be the promised land).

A carnal frenzy flushed my veins
(though at the risk of a stomach ache
I reasoned it wise to quell my yearnings
until my incipient
Lolita blossomed more fully).

The wait:
interminable biding
between introduction and consummation
drove me mad.
Chipping eternity with a toothpick,
a pious vigil I stood.

She emerged,
at last,
from pubescent incubation,
tan and mature,
secreting
(excreting)
a sensuality unparalleled
(by this time I couldn't tell which end was up).

Out of control
I possessed her,
devoured her,
consumed her every morsel
(something a lover should never do).

All that remained
of the epicurean carnage
(my infatuation)
was stuck to the tip of my chin.

"Mrs. Anderson,
pass me a napkin, please,
and will you bake another pie?"

And the secret is as follows.

–Sour Cream Apple Pie–

9-inch unbaked pie shell

–Filling–

⅔ cup sugar
2 tablespoons flour
½ teaspoon salt
1 cup sour cream
2 eggs, lightly beaten
½ teaspoon vanilla
3–4 cups thinly sliced apples

–Topping–

⅓ cup butter
⅓ cup flour
⅓ cup brown sugar
1 teaspoon cinnamon

With a fork, combine dry filling ingredients. Add sour cream, eggs, and vanilla. Fold in apples. Pour into pie shell and bake at 375° for 20 minutes or until apple mixture is set. Remove from oven and sprinkle with topping, which has been crumbled together with fork. Return to oven and bake for 8 minutes or until topping has melted. Serves 6.

–Apple Dumplings–

Apple dumplings are another simple, delicious dessert using Washington's best known export. The chopped filling may be used, or else the whole apple can be cored, wrapped in a pastry blanket, dotted with cinnamon and butter, covered with syrup, and baked.

Dough for double crust pie

–Filling–

1 cup apples, peeled and chopped
⅓ cup brown sugar
½ teaspoon cinnamon
butter

—Syrup

4 tablespoons butter
1 cup brown sugar
½ cup water

Chill pie dough and divide into 6 pieces. Roll each piece into a circle to ⅛ inch thick and spread center with filling, made up of apples, sugar, and cinnamon, mixed together. Dot with butter and fold edges of dough carefully over filling and pinch to completely seal apple mixture. Dot with butter and place side by side in greased square baking pan. Bake at 350° for 20 minutes.

In small saucepan heat butter, brown sugar, and water to boiling and pour over dumplings. Bake 20 minutes or until dough is golden brown and syrup bubbles thickly. Serves 4.

—Apple Cake

Apples seem to inspire family recipes. This cake has been in my family for four generations and has been made with apples grown in Georgia, South Carolina, Pennsylvania, Ohio, and Washington. Uncommonly moist and delicious, this recipe deserves to be sent around the country from one good kitchen to another.

1½ cups oil
1 cup brown sugar
1 cup white sugar
3 eggs
2 teaspoons vanilla
3 cups flour
1 teaspoon soda
½ teaspoon baking powder
½ teaspoon salt
2 teaspoons grated orange rind
4 large apples, coarsely chopped
1 cup walnuts or pecans, chopped

Mix oil, sugar, eggs, and vanilla, and beat until smooth. Add flour, soda, baking powder, salt, and orange rind, and stir until thoroughly blended. Add apples and nuts and mix well. Pour into well-greased tube cake pan or 2 loaf pans. Bake at 350° for 1 hour or until toothpick stuck into center comes out clean. Serve warm or cold. Serves 12.

–Apple Fritters

Apple fritters bring back fond childhood memories of wonderful smells in the kitchen and a plate full of goodies sitting out on top of the stove.

For the successful completion of this recipe, it is important to make sure that the cooking fat is hot enough. 400° is perfect.

1⅓ cups flour
2 teaspoons baking powder
¼ teaspoon salt
⅔ cup milk
1 egg, well beaten
6 medium apples, peeled and sliced
Cooking oil for frying
Confectioner's sugar

Mix dry ingredients, gradually add milk, and stir in egg. Add apple slices and stir until well blended. Drop mixture by spoonfuls into hot fat. When puffed up and brown, remove from fat and drain on paper towel. Keep warm in 250° oven and serve sprinkled with confectioner's sugar. Serves 6.

–Apple Custard

Because of an unending supply of fresh cream and milk, I seem to make a lot of custards. This apple variation of the classic custard recipe is delightful and can be garnished with thick slices of whole fruit, which can be kept from darkening by dropping them into a mixture of water and fresh lemon juice.

6 egg yolks
½ cup sugar
1 cup applesauce
¼ cup apple cider or juice
1 teaspoon lemon extract
1 cup milk
Apple slices
Whipped cream

Put egg yolks, sugar, applesauce, and apple juice in top of double boiler and stir over high heat until smooth. Add lemon extract and milk, and continue cooking—beating with whisk until thickened, usually about 20 minutes.

Pour into custard cups, chill, and garnish with apple slices and whipped cream. Serves 8.

–Apple Chutney

Apple jelly, apple butter, and especially apple chutney are all good ways to preserve apples once the freezer is full of applesauce. Chutneys can be varied to include all sorts of spices, in addition to those suggested in this recipe.

2 cups apple cider vinegar
2 lbs. brown sugar
2 lbs. tart apples, peeled
  and coarsely chopped
1 tablespoon fresh ginger, scraped
  and finely chopped
2 cloves garlic, peeled and finely chopped
1 tablespoon salt
1 teaspoon cayenne

Pour vinegar into a Dutch oven, add sugar, and stir over medium heat until sugar dissolves. Add remaining ingredients and reduce heat to low. Stir mixture gently, but constantly, until apples are soft, but not broken. Seal in sterilized jars. Makes about 4 pints.

—Apples Stuffed— with Yams

This recipe is a variation of the traditional baked apple. The fruit should be scooped out well to allow plenty of room for the stuffing, but the bottom of the apple must remain intact.

8 medium apples, cored
  and scooped out in center
2 large yams, each cut into 3 pieces
4 tablespoons butter, softened
½ teaspoon cinnamon
1 cup brown sugar
½ cup water
1½ teaspoons fresh grated orange rind

Boil yams in large saucepan until tender, then peel and mash. Blend in butter and cinnamon and stir well. Fill apples with yam mixture and place them in square baking pan. In small saucepan, combine sugar, water, and orange rind. Simmer over medium heat until thick, then pour over apples. Top each apple with an additional bit of butter and bake at 350° for 30 minutes, basting occasionally, or until apples are soft. Serves 8.

—Apple-Cabbage Slaw—

It seems as though most people who enjoy good food have their own favorite slaw recipe. Here is mine.

½ medium green cabbage, shredded
½ small purple cabbage, shredded
2–3 stalks bok choy, chopped
1 golden beet, grated
4 tart apples, cored and diced
1 medium onion, chopped
1 cup carrots, coarsely grated

—Dressing

1 cup yogurt
½ cup mayonnaise
1 cup large-curd cottage cheese
⅓ cup apple cider vinegar
3 tablespoons honey
2 tablespoons poppy seeds
6 mint leaves, shredded
2 teaspoons celery seed

Combine vegetables and chill. Put yogurt, mayonnaise, cottage cheese, vinegar and honey in blender. Blend until thoroughly mixed and add poppy seeds, mint, and celery seed. Pour dressing over chilled vegetables and blend well. Serves 6.

—Mushroom Apple Sauté

I like mushroom apple sauté especially well when chanterelles are in season and can be found in nearby woods. During the rest of the year, though, domestic mushrooms are a satisfactory substitute and often supply a more palatable texture to the end result.

¾ lb. mushrooms, clean and thinly sliced
3 tablespoons butter
3 medium tart apples, peeled and thinly sliced
1½ teaspoons sage, crushed or ground

Melt butter and sauté mushrooms in medium frying pan over moderate heat for 10 minutes or until liquid in pan has nearly evaporated. Add sliced apples, sprinkle with sage, and cook, stirring frequently, until apples begin to soften. Use additional butter if mixture seems too dry. Serves 6.

MUSHROOM HUNTING

One great thing about searching for mushrooms in the fall is that the weather almost never interferes—in fact, the damper and more miserable the outdoor conditions become, the more likely it is that there will be a bountiful supply blanketing forests and meadows throughout the region west of the Cascades. I've been told that there are more varieties of mushrooms in greater numbers in the Puget Sound area than anywhere else in the country. So for the legions of local mushroom hunters who take their hobby seriously, the Pacific Northwest is heaven on earth.

I count several of those dedicated souls among my closest friends, but for years their devotion to the hunt puzzled me. One or two trips into the woods, however, and I quickly learned the reasons for such boundless enthusiasm. There is something purely magic about finding a chanterelle, for example, tucked under a blueberry bush and almost hidden by fallen fir needles. Once found, cut, and put into a bag, the chanterelle (or any one of dozens of other species) becomes an even greater treasure when it is used in superb pies and sauces and stuffings in the kitchen.

One of my favorite forests to prowl for mushrooms is a couple of hours southeast of Seattle, not far from the eastern boundary of Olympic National Park. There are several large lakes lined with resort homes in this area, but most of the countryside is sparsely populated and devoted to timber cultivation. The virgin forests have long since disappeared, but the companies that own the land replant vigorously, so that tall fir and cedar are always available for systematic harvest.

Fall mushrooms may turn up as early as Labor Day weekend, but are more likely to appear in late September. The season usually continues for several months or until a good frost comes and fruiting ceases. During the season, the moderately intrepid hunter can easily gather enough of the choicest specimens to fill a home dryer or canner at least once, and so ensure wonderful culinary adventures during most of the year.

We left fairly early one rainy Saturday morning and planned to spend most of the day in pursuit of both the white chanterelle and the more common yellow chanterelle (Cantharellus subalbidus and C. cibarius). These distinctive mushrooms are some of the most delicious and versatile varieties around. Usually found on forest floors beneath lofty Douglas fir, the chanterelle will sometimes appear singly, but more frequently in groups of a dozen or more.

We drove quickly away from the last town between Seattle and our destina-
tion. All of a sudden the road became lined with several edible mushroom
varieties that we recognized, as well as with a few that we needed to look
up in our guidebook. A necessary accompaniment to any mushroom excur-
sion, a detailed, well-illustrated guide serves as a ready reference for both
the eager novice and the inquisitive expert. Even those who have hunted
mushrooms all of their lives still carry a guidebook, as the differences be-
tween certain edible and poisonous specimens are often minute.

The paved road finally ended and we drove cautiously along a deeply rut-
ted dirt extension. When the car could proceed no farther, we got out, but-
toned our raingear, and gathered up pocket knives and large plastic bags.
Here was The Spot, a small patch of forest that one of our party knew from
past experience to be particularly provident. A narrow break in the dense
undergrowth allowed entrance to the thickly treed area. Blueberry bushes
stood shoulder high, laden with ripe and juicy fruit. At our feet were the
objects of the journey—literally hundreds of chanterelles.

Within a few hours we had filled and refilled several bags. Since most of
the mushrooms had been at least partially hidden by fallen fir needles,
each specimen had to be scraped as clean as possible before being care-
fully placed in the gathering bag. The mushrooms were placed gills down
in the bag to prevent additional dirt from landing in the hard-to-clean un-
derside of the cap.

Mushrooms, at least wild ones, should never be washed, and so it is espe-
cially important to clean them as much as possible at the time of harvest.
Chanterelles have very little stem distinct from the cap, so they must be
trimmed particularly close to the ground, which often means that an ample
portion of dirt and leaves comes away along with the mushroom.

After lunch we returned to the woods to look for some different varieties to
*augment the chanterelle harvest. The king boletus (*Boletus edulis)*, which*
can grow to a height of ten inches with a cap almost a foot in diameter,
appeared again and again. These mushrooms tend to get wormy very
quickly and since only fresh specimens are desirable, it is important to
check each one carefully for pests, usually by slicing off a piece of the cap.

A highly prized eating mushroom in Europe, where it is known as cèpe, the
king boletus makes a fine addition to soups, sauces, and stuffings. It also
lends itself well to drying for use in subsequent months; in fact, this pro-
cess seems to enhance the mushroom's natural smoky flavor. Most mush-
rooms are best when every part of the stem and cap is used, but the tubes
under the cap of the boletus should be removed before eating. This spongy

material does not add to the mushroom's distinctive taste or otherwise firm texture, and it is a real handicap to proper drying.

*Certain mushrooms are prized for a particularly exotic flavor. One such favorite, known popularly as the prince (*Agaricus augustus*), greeted us boldly by the side of the road on the return home from the successful chanterelle expedition. The prince, which is not often very prolific, smells and tastes like almonds. We found an exceptionally fine specimen that afternoon, some eight inches across at the cap, and, as I bent to lift it into the bag, one of my friends suddenly noticed two others of similar dimension and apparent freshness just down the hill.*

Upon returning from any successful gathering expedition, it is important to use the mushrooms rather quickly when fresh or to prepare them immediately for canning, freezing, or drying. The simplest preparation is often the best. All edible mushrooms lend their delicate flavor nicely to a quick sauté in a bit of butter. Once sautéed, almost any mushroom goes well into a simple white sauce or omelet.

Even mushrooms with great keeping qualities will not last much more than a week in the refrigerator. One easy method of preserving them is to sauté small quantities and freeze meal-size portions in plastic containers. Canning with a good spicy marinade also works well. But I prefer to dry most of the mushrooms earmarked for preservation. By using a simple, homemade dryer, one can preserve many pounds of fresh mushrooms with little resultant need for storage space. Several dozen pounds of thinly sliced mushrooms will dry in three or four days.

It is also important to use any particular mushroom in a variety of ways in order to experience its full culinary potential. Of course, any of the recipes included in this chapter can be made with the grocery shelf Agaricus bisporus. *The results are good, but not nearly as interesting as when wild varieties are used.*

Chanterelles

Chanterelles are thought by many to be the most versatile of the commonly found wild mushrooms. Sautéed and served as a side dish with fowl or red meat, or featured in a meatless main dish, the chanterelle is an unforgettable eating experience. A bit of lemon juice seems to bring out this mushroom's distinctive taste, no matter how it is then prepared.

─Chanterelle Pie─────

One of my favorite mushroom meals features chanterelle pie in a cream cheese crust. This recipe is the first I ever prepared using wild mushrooms, and it made me a true believer.

─Crust────────────────

8-oz. package cream cheese,
   at room temperature
½ cup butter, at room temperature
1½ cups white flour

─Filling──────────────

3 lbs. chanterelles, thinly sliced
2 tablespoons butter
1 medium white onion, sliced
1 teaspoon salt
½ teaspoon freshly ground black pepper
1 teaspoon fresh parsley
   or ½ teaspoon ground sage
2 tablespoons lemon juice
1 cup sour cream

Break cream cheese and butter into small pieces and combine thoroughly with flour until soft dough is formed. Divide dough into 2 fist-size balls and chill for 15 minutes, then roll out into 2 ⅛-inch crusts.

Sauté mushrooms in butter in medium frying pan over medium heat until most of liquid has evaporated. Add onion and cook, stirring occasionally, until limp. Sprinkle with salt, pepper, parsley or sage, and lemon juice, and stir well. Remove from heat and stir in sour cream.

Place one crust into 9-inch pie pan. Pour in mushroom mixture. Seal with top crust, slashing several times in center. Bake at 375° for 40 minutes or until crust is brown. Serves 6.

–Chanterelle Pizza

Mushrooms are often the basis for meatless main dishes. One such dish, this pizza can be augmented and varied with all sorts of vegetables. The essential ingredient is the chanterelles.

–Crust

1 teaspoon baking yeast
⅔ cup warm water
1 tablespoon sugar
1½–2 cups white flour
¼ teaspoon salt
1 teaspoon baking powder

–Filling

2 tablespoons butter
2 cups chanterelles
1 small garlic clove, mashed
1 tablespoon lemon juice
1 small can tomato paste
½ teaspoon fresh basil
½ teaspoon dried oregano
½ cup pitted black olives, chopped
1 green pepper, thinly sliced
1 medium onion, sliced
4 green chilies, cut in thin strips
1½ cups grated Cheddar cheese
1½ cups grated mozzarella or jack cheese

Combine yeast and water thoroughly and add sugar. Mix 1½ cups flour, salt, and baking powder, then add yeast mixture and blend until soft dough begins to form. Knead until smooth, adding flour as necessary, and set dough aside to rest.

Melt butter and sauté mushrooms with garlic and lemon juice in medium frying pan. Lightly oil pizza pan or baking sheet. Coat dough with a thin film of oil and stretch it over pan, making a lip at edge to prevent filling from spilling over.

Spread dough evenly with tomato paste and sprinkle with basil and oregano. Spoon mushrooms evenly over crust and top with olives and vegetables. Sprinkle with cheeses and bake at 450° for 20 minutes or until bottom of crust is brown. Serves 4.

–Curried Chanterelles–

Another tasty main dish features chanterelles flavored with curry. This can be served over rice with traditional curry condiments, such as chopped cashews and scallions or grated carrot. Homemade chutney is also highly recommended.

2 medium onions, thinly sliced
3 tablespoons butter
1 medium garlic clove, mashed
2 cups chopped tomatoes
3 cups chicken or vegetable stock
1 tablespoon curry powder
Dash cayenne
1 teaspoon salt
1 lb. chanterelles, chopped into large chunks
½ cup currants, boiled until plump

In medium frying pan, sauté onion in butter and garlic until golden, then add tomatoes. Simmer lightly until liquid is reduced by half. Then add stock, seasonings, mushrooms, and currants. Simmer for 15 minutes. Serves 2.

–Marinated–
Chanterelles

Chanterelles can be easily dried, or sautéed and frozen, but the best method of preservation, according to many mushroom experts, is marinating and then canning. Once marinated for several months, these mushrooms can be used for the rest of the year as hors d'oeuvres or in salads. The longer they soak, the better their flavor.

3 lbs. chanterelles
6 cups tarragon vinegar
1 cup lemon juice
3 lemons, sliced
2 cups olive oil
2 tablespoons salt
8 peppercorns
Dash Tabasco sauce
3 large garlic cloves, minced
2 cups chopped onion
⅓ cup chopped parsley
2 bay leaves
1 teaspoon fennel seed

Trim, brush, and wipe mushrooms. If large, slice into chunks, leave whole if small. Blanch for 3 minutes and drain immediately.

In Dutch oven bring remaining ingredients to a boil. Add mushrooms and simmer for 30 minutes. Seal in clean quart jars and process in boiling water bath for 15 minutes. Age 2 months before use. Makes approximately 3 quarts.

Boletus

Zesty boletus—especially the king—adds substance and savor to otherwise ordinary soups and stews. When the mushrooms are dried, they can be reconstituted remarkably well by a 15-minute soaking in water.

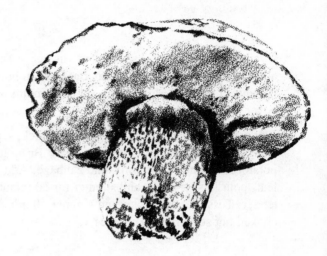

–Boletus-Vegetable– Soup

This fall garden soup gains a distinctive and unusual flavor when boletus are added.

4 lbs. chicken parts
4 quarts water
1 tablespoon vinegar
1 tablespoon salt
10 peppercorns
1 cup dried boletus
1 cup diced carrots
1 cup diced potatoes
1 medium onion, cut into chunks
1 cup shredded cabbage
1 small garlic clove, minced
1 teaspoon thyme
1 tablespoon soy sauce
Bay leaf
1 cup chopped green beans

Combine chicken parts, water, and vinegar in Dutch oven or stockpot, and add salt and peppercorns. Simmer at least an hour, uncovered, until liquid is reduced by half. Meanwhile, set mushrooms aside in a small bowl and cover with water.

Remove chicken and peppercorns from stock, separate meat from bones and return, chopped into bitesize pieces. Bring it to a boil, adding carrots, potatoes, onion, mushrooms, and cabbage. Add garlic, thyme, and bay leaf, pour in soy sauce, and simmer for 20 minutes or until potatoes are tender. Toss in green beans and simmer 10 minutes more or until beans are cooked but still crunchy. Serves 4.

–Boletus and Pear Sauce

Boletus also combine nicely with fruit. This sauce can be served over saffron rice, but it is highly recommended over spinach- or cheese-filled crepes.

1 quart dried boletus
2 cups cream
½ cup dry sherry
4 small pears, peeled and cut into chunks
½ teaspoon fresh summer savory
      ***or* ½ teaspoon crushed coriander leaves (cilantro)**
Salt and pepper

Soak mushrooms in water for several hours, changing water frequently. Slice mushrooms into strips and simmer in medium frying pan in cream and sherry for 10 minutes. Add pears, savory or coriander, and salt and pepper to taste. Stir once and serve, garnished with chopped savory or coriander leaves. Serves 4.

Agaricus

Due in part to their mild and often subtle flavor, the agaricus varieties are usually considered the most delicious of wild mushrooms, at least by the untrained palate. The prince (Agaricus augustus) tops the list for flavor and is often quite large. One giant specimen can easily provide the substance of dinner for four.

–Mushroom Crepes

This simple white sauce enables both the flavor and texture of this wonderful mushroom to be fully experienced. Crab is a tasty addition.

— Crepe Batter

½ cup light cream
½ cup water
2 eggs
1 cup white flour
2 tablespoons butter, melted
¼ teaspoon salt

— Filling

½ cup butter
3 tablespoons flour
1½ cups light cream
½ cup dry white wine
1 lb. prince mushrooms, sliced
¼ teaspoon salt
¼ lb. Dungeness crabmeat

To make crepe batter, pour cream, water, and eggs into blender, and beat until smooth. Then add flour, butter, and salt, and beat until thoroughly blended. Chill for at least one hour prior to use.

To make filling, melt 4 tablespoons butter in top of a double boiler and stir in flour, cooking over medium heat for several minutes while stirring continually. Add cream, beat well, and simmer for 15 minutes or until thickened. Then add wine and stir until smooth.

In medium frying pan, sauté mushrooms in remaining butter and salt.

When tender but still firm, add to sauce and stir. Then add crab and keep sauce warm over low heat.

To make crepes, use medium frying pan or crepe pan. Heat pan until a drop of water evaporates immediately, then place 1 tablespoon butter in pan and swirl it to coat bottom. Working quickly, pour several tablespoons of batter into center of pan, then lift from burner and tilt pan back and forth so that batter spreads evenly. Crepe is ready to turn when sides come away from edges of pan, usually after about 2 minutes over medium high heat. Cook second side briefly and remove crepe from pan.

Ladle filling into crepes and roll them up. Serve warm. Makes 6 large crepes, serves 3–4.

–Mushroom Rösti–––––

Rösti is a Swiss invention that makes excellent use of leftover vegetables. The essence of several different vegetables combines well with almost any type of agaricus mushroom. Again the prince is the recommended choice, primarily for its distinctive flavor.

2 cups diced potatoes with skins
¾ cup butter
1 cup prince mushrooms, thinly sliced
1 medium onion, sliced
1 cup cooked vegetables, such as eggplant,
**   cauliflower, or zucchini**
Salt and pepper
Sour cream
Chopped chives

In small saucepan, cook potatoes in 1 cup water until tender. Sauté mushrooms and onion in medium frying pan in 4 tablespoons butter, until mushrooms are tender, but still firm. Push mushrooms and onions to one side of pan and add remaining butter to melt. Then add potatoes, vegetables, and salt and pepper to taste. Stir well and cook for 10 minutes over medium heat or until potatoes are golden. Serve with dollop of sour cream and sprinkling of chives. Serves 4.

Meadow Mushrooms

A relative of the prince, the meadow mushroom (Agaricus campestris) makes a frequent appearance on Puget Sound tables during the fall. Aptly named, this mushroom flourishes in nearby fields and pastures and is among the most accessible of any wild variety. Meadow mushrooms are best when very fresh, and their freshness is indicated by the presence of bright pink gills. They are an excellent substitute for domestic mushrooms in any recipe.

Meadow mushrooms are often added to pot roasts and other basic meat dishes, but they may also be successfully used with chicken and other fowl. The two following recipes treat the mushroom differently and both achieve excellent results.

–Mushroom-Green— Bean Vinaigrette

1 lb. fresh green beans, steamed
and sliced in long thin strips
½ lb. meadow mushrooms, thinly sliced
1 small onion, chopped
2 eggs, hardboiled and chopped fine
1 cup yogurt
2 tablespoons olive oil
2 tablespoons tarragon vinegar
1 teaspoon fresh lemon juice
½ teaspoon Dijon mustard
1 teaspoon honey
Salt and pepper

Place beans, mushrooms, onion, and eggs in large bowl. In another bowl, combine yogurt, oil, vinegar, lemon juice, mustard, and honey, and stir well. Add salt and pepper to taste. Pour yogurt mixture over beans and cover. Store in refrigerator for 2 days, stirring occasionally. Serves 4.

–Mushroom Fritters

½ lb. meadow mushrooms, sliced
2 tablespoons oil
4 tablespoons butter, melted
½ teaspoon soy sauce
6 eggs, separated
2 cups large-curd cottage cheese
½ cup white flour
¼ teaspoon salt

In medium frying pan, sauté mushrooms in oil and half of butter and soy sauce until liquid has nearly evaporated. Set aside. Blend egg yolks, cottage cheese, and remaining butter. Add flour and salt, and stir well. Then fold in stiffly beaten egg whites and carefully blend in mushrooms. Drop by spoonfuls onto hot greased griddle and fry until golden. Serves 2.

Pine Mushrooms

*The pine mushroom or matsutake (*Armillaria ponderosa*) is gathered in great quantities by Japanese cooks and others who love Oriental food. A most versatile and savory mushroom, matsutake stores well when just picked and keeps best for later use when canned. It is used in a number of traditional meals—including sukiyaki and many stir-fried dishes. This mushroom is also an excellent addition to the stuffing for almost any fowl. The stems of most matsutake are rather tough, however, and so should be diagonally sliced very thin before use.*

–Matsutake Salmon

This recipe combines two of the Northwest's most delicious naturally abundant foods—matsutake and salmon—for a spectacular result.

3 medium matsutake, thinly sliced
3 tablespoons butter
5 small zucchini, thinly sliced
2 cups sour cream
¾ cup dry sherry
½ teaspoon dried dill weed
½ teaspoon salt

½ **teaspoon black pepper**
2 **lbs. salmon cutlets or fillets**

In medium frying pan, sauté mushrooms in half of butter for 20 minutes or until very tender. Put to one side and sauté zucchini in remaining butter for 5 minutes or until tender.

Blend sour cream, sherry, dill, salt, and pepper. Place salmon in large baking pan, cover with vegetables, and pour sauce over top. Bake at 400° for 20 minutes. Serves 6.

HUNTING FOR DEER AND ELK

There are thousands of hunters in the Pacific Northwest who set out with guns every fall in hopes of shooting a deer or an elk, but only a relative few head into the mountains armed only with bows and arrows. Bow hunters take themselves very seriously, and the state has provided special areas and seasons for them to pursue their sport. Unlike those who hunt with guns, bow hunters rely on skill as much as luck. And the skillful often come home with a prize.

One hunter I know still talks about his first success with a bow several seasons ago. Setting up camp at a moderate elevation in the Cascades, he rose early the next morning to hike several miles to the top of a nearby ridge where he hoped to spot a deer. Dressed in Army camouflage, he reached a small lake and found a good vantage point from which he could see most of the surrounding forest. He sat quietly in the underbrush beneath the spruce and fir, effectively hidden from view, and waited for a deer.

After several hours, he suddenly heard a lot of noise and looked up to see a wolf chasing a large black-tail deer a few hundred yards away. The hunter cocked his bow, shot, and his arrow hit the deer squarely in the neck. He then dropped quietly to his knees and waited for the wounded deer to collapse. The thrashing suddenly subsided after a few minutes and the hunter began his search for the dying animal. He carefully made his way through the undergrowth and, without warning, he suddenly dropped over a ledge and fell about ten feet. Unhurt by the fall, which was broken by several clumps of scraggly bushes, the hunter looked up from the spot where he had landed and saw the deer just a few feet away. It had apparently taken the same fall he had. Elated by his good fortune, the hunter quickly killed his prize and began the long trek back down to his camp.

The 120-pound buck was on its way to a kitchen eager for venison.

There are three types of deer in Washington; all are heavily hunted. The black-tail deer is found throughout western Washington, where it feeds on woody plants, berry leaves, and other undergrowth. Black-tail were not common in the area until heavy logging of mountain forests allowed their food sources to flourish on clearcut slopes and in flat open areas. These deer also indulge in cultivated crops such as alfalfa, oats, and wheat— much to the displeasure of local farmers. They are hunted today to keep the population from overwhelming its food source.

White-tail deer account for some 10 percent of the annual deer harvest in Washington. They are found in the northeastern corner of the state as well as in the opposite corner along the Columbia River. This deer, like the black-tail, prefers dense forests and is somewhat more difficult to capture than the mule deer, which lives in open areas throughout eastern Washington. Both the white-tail and the mule deer eat forage foods that grow wild or are cultivated.

Elk are not hunted so actively or successfully as deer. There are two sub-species in Washington—the Roosevelt in the western Cascade mountains and Olympic range and the Rocky Mountains east of the Cascade summit. Elk are gregarious and gather in herds of five to twenty. They feed almost totally on grass and forage.

Most hunters realize that good field care is essential to bringing home good meat. The animal must be bled promptly and carefully eviscerated. The carcass must also be allowed to cool before being packed into an en-closed area such as the trunk of a car. After these simple rules have been followed, it is off to the butcher for hanging, cutting, and wrapping.

Both venison and elk have lean and dry meat that often needs to be larded or marinated to achieve the best flavor and texture. The quality of the meat is dependent on the age of the animal.

—Venison Chops—

Chops from a young deer can be surprisingly tender, especially when sautéed and then simmered in a mildly seasoned sauce.

6 venison chops
3 tablespoons butter
¼ teaspoon thyme
¼ teaspoon garlic powder
Salt and pepper
½ cup red wine
½ cup beef bouillon

In large frying pan, melt butter and sauté chops over moderate heat for several minutes on each side until lightly and evenly browned. Sprinkle with seasonings and pour in wine and bouillon. Reduce heat to low and simmer for 10 minutes. Serves 4.

—Venison Roast—

This venison roast recipe came from a professional cook who, over the last thirty years, has served almost as much venison as beef. Although any cut of meat can be used, the long marinating process is especially effective for the tougher portions of the animal.

3-lb. venison roast
1 cup sliced mushrooms
2½ cups beef bouillon
1 cup dry red wine
2 garlic cloves, minced
⅔ cup onion, finely chopped
½ teaspoon basil
½ cup flour
1½ teaspoon salt
¼ teaspoon pepper
¼ teaspoon thyme
¼ teaspoon basil
½ teaspoon paprika
¼ cup vegetable oil

Place meat and mushrooms in large bowl and regularly pierce entire surface of meat with a fork. Mix bouillon, wine, garlic, onion, and basil, and pour over meat. Be sure that meat is covered with liquid (add water if necessary) and refrigerate for 3 days.

Remove meat from marinade and dry thoroughly. Reserve marinade. Combine flour, salt, pepper, thyme, basil, and paprika. Coat meat with mixture and brown in oil in a Dutch oven. Pour marinade over meat and cover. Bake at 350° for 3 hours or until tender. Serves 6.

—Venison Sausage—

Sausage is a great way to use the venison packages that return from the butcher marked "ground." The tough cuts can be ground at home for use in sausage as well.

> **3 lbs. ground venison**
> **1 lb. ground fresh pork**
> **5 teaspoons salt**
> **2 teaspoons pepper**
> **½ teaspoon ground cloves**
> **1 teaspoon sugar**
> **4 tablespoons sage**

Mix all ingredients together. Makes 2 dozen patties.

—Pepper Jelly—

Pepper jelly, a traditional and delicious condiment for game, is especially popular in the South. This recipe was passed on to me by a Southern cousin who loves to cook. I hope to make it a Northwest tradition as well.

> **6½ cups sugar**
> **¾ cup green peppers, minced**
> **½ cup hot red chili peppers, minced**
> **1½ cup cider vinegar**
> **6 ounces liquid pectin**

Bring sugar, peppers, and vinegar to a boil in medium saucepan, and boil for 1 minute. Remove from heat and let stand briefly, then add pectin and pour into clean pint jars. Makes 4 pints.

HUNTING FOR GAME BIRDS

Hunting wild game and game birds was hardly recreational activity for the early pioneers in Washington and Oregon, who depended greatly on their marksmanship to keep food on the table. The natural plenty of the Northwest was one of the major attractions to new settlers, and—although the arrival and breeding of domestic animals was greeted eagerly as a sign of "civilization"—venison, elk, grouse, and dove remained standard fare in many households.

Today's hunters are similarly eager, albeit for different reasons. The camaraderie among partners, the occasional opportunity to weekend in a remote area of the state, and the promise of tasty dinners for the successful make hunting very popular on both sides of the Cascades. So-called upland game birds thrive in most of the different geographical regions of the Northwest, and migratory fowl are present in great numbers along the Pacific Flyway.

The Skagit Flats, some sixty miles north of Seattle, attract duck hunters by the hundreds, as do the Nisqually Flats forty miles south. The Columbia River Basin provides cover and food for ducks and geese in central Washington. The area around Moses Lake with its Potholes Recreation Area is especially popular. The Willamette Valley is home for even more ducks and geese in Oregon. Both game birds and ducks can be foond in almost every county of both states.

The most common native upland game birds are several different varieties of grouse, some found in wet forested areas and others in sagebrush-covered hills. Mourning doves, considered by many to be the tastiest of game birds, are also very common in eastern Washington. The band-tailed pigeon lives west of the Cascades and is heavily hunted there.

The most popular game bird in the state, as well as throughout America, is the Chinese or Ringnecked Pheasant. This bird was introduced to America in 1880 by Judge O. N. Denny, who shipped seventy of them to his brother John, who lived in the Willamette Valley. Most of that shipment died quickly, as did another, but a third group arrived in good condition in 1883. Many of those birds were released to thrive on Protection Island near the entrance to Puget Sound. These Denny imports and several others from China provided the nucleus of today's resident pheasant population.

Wild turkey and several varieties of quail and partridge have also been introduced in the Northwest with great success. The chukar partridge is a favorite with hunters because of long hunting seasons, liberal bag limits, and its general fondness for the dry desert drainage areas of the major rivers of western Washington.

Although many hunt geese, ducks are the most eagerly sought of the migratory waterfowl. Five major species are found in Washington; mallard, sprig, widgeon, wood duck, and teal. Many of these birds nest in Alaska and Canada and head south to the warmer climate of Washington and Oregon for the winter.

Flocks of widgeon appear in the late fall and winter to feed around golf courses, park lawns, and pastures with nearby ponds. Teal are more often found in marshes, as was the canvasback, a once common bird that has virtually disappeared with the destruction of its marshland habitat. The wood duck has become a local resident and will happily nest in an artificial nesting box.

Bird hunting opens in mid-October and runs as late as the end of January for some species. Licenses are required, and hunting laws are strictly enforced. Bag limits vary from two for pheasants in western Washington to ten for quail in eastern Washington. So the successful hunter who doubles as or supplies a skillful cook can bring in two weeks worth of game-bird dinners with a weekend's honest effort.

Preparation of Game Birds

Game birds must have their feathers removed, and be cleaned and "hung" for several days before cooking. These procedures are rather routine and sometimes tedious, but they must be done carefully.

Although the feathers can be removed by dipping the bird in hot water or paraffin, one expert I know prefers the simple dry plucking method. He simply dons a pair of rubber gloves and plucks a few feathers at a time by pulling them in the direction of the tail. The effectiveness of this method is a result of the high oil content of both duck and goose feathers. The friction created by the lateral motion of two fingers rubbed along the skin enables even the smallest feathers and down to come free with ease.

Since the bird is drawn or bled before plucking, the remaining task is to eviscerate it. The crop, located in the throat, should first be cut away. A second incision across the breastbone and across the vent or hind end will allow for the easy removal of the entrails. The emptied cavity should then be thoroughly washed and meticulously cleaned. Poultry shears can then be used to snip away the wing tips and feet. The bird can then be stored in the refrigerator for one or two days in order to tenderize the meat and improve its flavor.

The way birds should be cooked depends on their size, age, and condition. A large duck, usually a mallard, may weigh 1½ to 2 pounds, but most ducks weigh a pound or less. Pheasants, of course, are larger, as are geese. Regardless of size, though, all game birds have dry flesh compared to that of domestic fowl and so require barding, or draping with bacon or salt pork, to keep them moist if they are to be roasted. If the bird is old (over a year in age), or in poor condition from the kill, it is likely that the cook will only use the breast pieces, cut into chunks, and make a curry or stew. Bones can be used for soup or to make stock.

The most important rule of game-bird cookery is to avoid overcooking, which dries and toughens the meat and causes it to lose flavor. When roasting a bird, the meat should be tested for doneness at regular intervals. When there is more than one bird in the oven, each should be checked individually since cooking time can vary greatly. As a rule, though, roast pheasant will require about 25 minutes per pound and ducks will need 18 to 20 minutes per pound.

–Roast Duck

**4 mallards, widgeon, or sprig (about 1½ lbs.
  each), cleaned, plucked, and hung
4 tablespoons butter, softened
2 medium onions, cut into chunks
2–3 tart apples, peeled, cored, and diced
1 teaspoon sage
  or 36 juniper berries
16 slices bacon
3 garlic cloves, mashed
Freshly ground black pepper
Ground cloves
Parsley flakes**

Rinse ducks thoroughly inside and out, dry well, and rub cavity with butter. Stuff cavity with onions and apples mixed with sage or juniper berries, then more onions. Sew cavity shut or close it with skewers. Rub bacon slices with garlic and sprinkle lightly with cloves, pepper, and parsley flakes. With toothpicks, pin bacon barding over bird by running one slice along breastbone and three more across the breastbone. Tie well with kitchen string or dental floss to prevent bacon from curling during roasting.

Put birds on poultry rack in long baking pan and place in preheated 500°

oven. Immediately reduce heat to 325° and cook for 40 minutes or until flesh has just turned from red to pink at thickest part. Check doneness at 25 minutes and every 5 minutes thereafter to avoid overcooking. Serves 8.

–Orange Roast–
Pheasant

Pheasants can be roasted in the same way as ducks (see above recipe) or with this delicious orange glaze. The legs should also be barded, since pheasant, unlike duck, has some meat on the legs. This glaze makes barding unnecessary, however, and still keeps the meat moist.

2 pheasant, cut into quarters
3 tablespoons butter
1 cup orange marmalade
4 ounces Cointreau

In large frying pan, sauté pheasant pieces in melted butter over low heat for 5 minutes or until lightly browned on both sides. Place in long baking pan and cover with well-blended mixture of marmalade and Cointreau, and put into preheated 500° oven. Immediately reduce heat to 325° and bake for 35 minutes or until done. Baste frequently and check for doneness after 20 minutes in the oven and every 5 minutes thereafter. Serves 4.

–Curried Stuffing–

The apple-and-onion stuffing from the roast duck or pheasant is often rather tasteless when cooked and is not usually served. But this savory curry stuffing is well worth trying; it can bake in the oven along with the birds.

4 tablespoons butter
2 cups chopped celery
1 cup chopped onion
½ medium apple, chopped
1 tablespoon sugar
1 tablespoon curry powder
4 cups stale bread cubes
¾ cup chicken stock

In medium frying pan melt butter and sauté celery and onion until golden. Add apple, sugar, and curry powder, and cook over moderate heat until apple is tender but firm. Add to bread cubes and moisten mixture with chicken stock. Bake in small Dutch oven, uncovered, at 325° for 20 minutes or until top is crisp. Serves 6.

–Classic Orange Sauce

Roast game birds are simply wonderful when covered with orange sauce. This classic method results in a mild version with an intentionally bitter flavor. The ersatz version in the next recipe is altogether different—very sweet, very orange.

> 1 cup game stock
> *or* 1 cup water, reserving 2 tablespoons
> flavored with 1 cube beef bouillon,
> 1 cube chicken bouillon, and
> ¼ teaspoon dried parsley
> *and* ¼ teaspoon dried thyme
> 1 tablespoon cornstarch
> 4 tablespoons vinegar
> 3 tablespoons sugar
> 1 tablespoon thinly sliced candied orange rind
> 1 cup heated orange juice
> 2 teaspoons lemon juice
> 4 tablespoons Cointreau or Grand Marnier
> 3 large oranges, peeled and sectioned

Remove cooked game birds from pan and pour in stock or flavored water and mix with juices and pan drippings from birds. Pour resulting mixture into small saucepan. Put vinegar and sugar in another saucepan and simmer over moderate heat until syrupy. Pour syrup into stock and simmer for 5 minutes. Combine cornstarch and reserved stock. Add to syrup and stock mixture, cooking over moderate heat until liquid thickens to coat spoon. Add rind, orange juice, and lemon juice, and simmer for 3 minutes. Adjust texture by stirring in more cornstarch if necessary. Stir in liqueur and pour over birds. Garnish with orange sections. Makes 1½ cups sauce.

–Very Orange Sauce–

1 cup game stock
  ***or* 1 10-oz. can chicken stock,**
  reserving 2 tablespoons
1 tablespoon cornstarch
1 cup bitter orange marmalade
½ cup orange juice
4 oz. Cointreau

In medium saucepan, pour in stock, add pan drippings from roast birds, and stir. Simmer over medium heat, beating until thickened. Combine reserved stock and cornstarch until smooth and add. Blend marmalade, orange juice, and liqueur, and add to thickened stock. Stir well and serve at once. Makes 2 cups.

–Pheasant in Sour– Cream Sauce

Although this recipe calls for pheasant, it also works very well with grouse or dove.

2 pheasants, cleaned and halved
1 teaspoon salt
¼ teaspoon freshly ground black pepper
½ cup flour
4 slices bacon
3 tablespoons butter
1 large onion, coarsely chopped
½ lb. mushrooms, thinly sliced
½ cup cooking sherry
1 garlic clove, mashed
3 tart apples, chopped
3 oz. applejack or brandy
1 cup sour cream
½ cup chicken stock

Sprinkle pheasant halves with salt and pepper, dredge in flour, and set aside. In large frying pan, fry bacon until crisp. Crumble cooked bacon and reserve for garnish. Pour off all but 1 tablespoon bacon fat, add 3 tablespoons of butter to pan, and lightly brown pheasant on both sides. Remove from pan and place in warm oven, covered to prevent drying out.

Sauté onions and mushrooms in pan until golden, then add sherry, garlic, and stir well. Return pheasant to pan and simmer for 10 minutes. Add ⅓ of the chopped apples and cook for 10 minutes over moderate heat. Add remaining apples and cook for 5 minutes more. Test for doneness and cook an additional 10 minutes if necessary.

In small saucepan combine applejack, sour cream, chicken stock and 1 tablespoon flour, and cook over low heat, stirring continually, for 5 minutes. Pour over pheasant and serve at once. Serves 4.

–Curried Duck–

Some birds come into the kitchen full of buckshot or otherwise unfit for cooking and serving whole or in large pieces. One hunter I know freezes such quantities of game birds that he often ends up with "old" ones. Both of these problems can be easily solved with this curry recipe, which uses small cubes of meat.

This is a sweet mild curry. For those who want a spicier result, the amount of curry powder can be doubled or tripled.

> **3 tablespoons butter**
> **4 cups duck meat, cut into ¾-inch cubes**
> **2 garlic cloves, minced**
> **3 medium onions, chopped**
> **1 3-inch piece fresh ginger**
> **2 tablespoons curry powder**
> **½ cup flour**
> **4 cups milk**
> **1 tablespoon cornstarch**
> **2 teaspoons salt**
> **2 cups heavy cream**
> **4 large fresh pineapple slices,**
> **   cut into bite-size pieces**
> **½ cup currants**
> **½ cup raisins**
> **½ cup green grapes**

Melt half the butter in large frying pan, add meat, and cook over moderate heat for 2 or 3 minutes or until evenly browned. In large saucepan melt

remaining butter, add garlic, onions, and gingerroot, and cook over low
heat for 20 minutes, stirring occasionally until onions are tender. Stir in
curry powder and flour and cook until all flour is absorbed by butter.
Gradually add 3 cups milk and cook until sauce thickens. Then combine
remaining milk and cornstarch and stir into sauce. Cook for several minutes, stirring constantly, and then add cream. Add fruit to sauce, then
meat, cover and cook over low heat for 15 minutes. Serve over brown rice.
Serves 8.

–Green Salsa––––––––

*Standard curry condiments, such as chopped bananas, raw cashews, or
grated zucchini should accompany the above recipe. This salsa is another
tasty complement.*

3 scallions, diced
1 medium green pepper, diced
3 sprigs parsley, coarsely chopped
½ cucumber, sliced very thin
2 medium tomatoes, chopped fine
3 tablespoons olive oil
Salt and pepper

Combine vegetables, mix well, and add just enough oil to coat evenly.
Sprinkle with salt and pepper to taste. Makes approximately 2 cups.

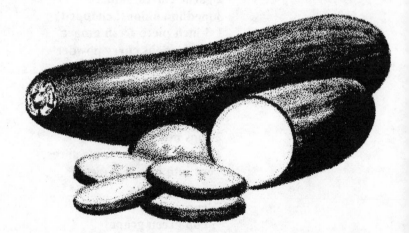

—Plum Pheasant————————

The secret to this very fruity pheasant dish is large, ripe, fat plums. Large Nubianas are the best, and they happen to be readily available in the Northwest, but other juicy varieties will do as well. Whatever the choice of fruit, it must be fresh.

2 pheasants, halved
3 tablespoons butter
1 cup water
2 tablespoons vinegar
2 tablespoons sugar
1 cup white seedless raisins
½ cup dried currants
1 cup chopped fresh pineapple
1½ cups green grapes, halved
1½ cups Concord grapes, halved
4 large or 6 medium plums

Melt butter in large frying pan and brown pheasant by cooking over medium heat for 3 minutes on each side. In large saucepan bring water to a boil, add vinegar and sugar, and stir until sugar dissolves. Then add fruit and reduce heat. Simmer for 10 minutes or until fruit softens. Pour sauce over pheasant and simmer slowly for 15 minutes or until pheasant is cooked. Serves 4.

LATE GARDEN VEGETABLES

My garden harvest generally falls into two different seasons, partly deter-mined by the elements and partly by staggered plantings throughout May and June. Harvest is always such a joyful experience that I try to make it last for as many weeks as possible.

By leaving some of the root crops in the ground, in storage so to speak, the carrot, beet, potato, and onion seasons last well into the fall, espe-cially if the weather is dry. Although many of the cole crops, especially broccoli and cauliflower, are finished off by the warm days of August and must be harvested as soon as they mature, cabbage, especially the red and purple varieties, will wait patiently for the cooler days of autumn before harvest. Then there are Brussels sprouts, with their unusually long grow-ing cycle, and winter squash and pumpkins that absolutely will not be rushed to maturity before October.

Green tomatoes will last until the first frost and are often considered a prize vegetable themselves. Since the harvest of red-ripe tomatoes is al-ways unpredictable west of the Cascades, most Pacific Northwesterners get plenty of practice turning green tomatoes into tasty pies, side dishes, relishes, and jam.

The final harvest is usually completed by late October and the garden is turned under for the winter with a spade or Roto-tiller. After a mild fall, though, I have been known to sit down to the Thanksgiving dinner table to eat creamed onions, green tomato pie, Brussels sprouts in cheese sauce, and pumpkin custard pie.

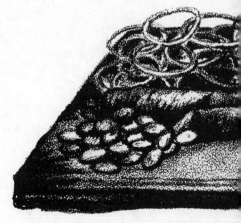

–Creamed Onions––––––––

Creamed onions are a Thanksgiving family tradition and one I anticipate joyfully year after year.

**1½ lbs. small boiling onions, peeled, sliced,
and separated into rings
3 tablespoons flour
1 teaspoon salt
¼ teaspoon nutmeg
4 tablespoons butter, melted
2 cups light cream
¾ cup bread crumbs**

In large saucepan heat 1 cup water to a boil and add onions. Cook for 3 to 5 minutes until tender. Place drained onions into square baking pan and sprinkle with flour, salt, and nutmeg. Cover onions with melted butter mixed with cream. Sprinkle with bread crumbs and bake at 350° for 30 minutes. Serves 6.

=Green Tomato Pie––––––––

Green tomato recipes are legion in the Pacific Northwest. They have even inspired at least one entire cookbook. A savory green tomato pie, replete with grated cheese and lots of fresh oregano, is a great addition to any bountiful fall table.

Crust for 9-inch pie

1 cup light cream
2 eggs
9 medium green tomatoes, peeled
and quartered
1 teaspoon salt
1 tablespoon fresh oregano
Dash cayenne
½ lb. Swiss cheese, coarsely grated

Beat cream and eggs until thoroughly blended. Place tomato quarters in bottom of pie shell. Pour liquid over tomatoes and sprinkle with salt, oregano, and cayenne. Cover with grated cheese and seal with top crust. Bake at 375° for 35 minutes or until brown. Serves 6.

–Green Tomato Chutney

Green tomato chutney is a staple in my house. It goes into omelets at breakfast, on sandwiches for lunch, and next to chicken, pork, or lamb at dinner.

2 cups water
2 cups apple cider vinegar
1 tablespoon salt
2 cups brown sugar
10 cups green tomatoes, coarsely chopped
3 large shallots, minced
2 medium white onions, coarsely chopped
3 cloves garlic, mashed
1 tablespoon celery seed
1 tablespoon fresh ginger, finely chopped
½ teaspoon cayenne
1 teaspoon ground cloves
3 tablespoons dark mustard seeds

In Dutch oven, place water, vinegar, salt, and sugar, and bring to a boil. Add tomatoes and simmer 15 minutes or until tender. Return to high heat and add shallots, onions, garlic, and spices. Simmer until thickened, stirring constantly for 20 minutes. Pack in sterilized jars or freeze. Makes 4 quarts.

Green Tomato Salsa

Green tomato salsa is a good taco sauce, relish with Mexican food, or seasoning for beans, soups, and stews.

¼ cup olive oil
8 quarts green tomatoes, chopped
6 green peppers, chopped
6 onions, chopped
8 cloves garlic, minced
3 tablespoons salt
1 tablespoon chili Tepinas, finely ground
1 tablespoon cumin
2 cups jalapeño peppers, chopped
3 tablespoons brown sugar
3 cups cider vinegar

Heat oil in large Dutch oven and sauté tomatoes, green peppers, onions, and garlic. Add salt, spices, jalapeños, sugar, and cider. Bring to a boil and boil slowly for about 3 hours. Pour into hot clean jars, seal, and process for 10 minutes in boiling water. Let stand for at least 3 weeks before using. Makes 8 pints.

Brussels Sprouts with Cheese Sauce

Brussels sprouts are one of the easiest vegetables to grow in a temperate climate, but they are often overlooked because they are supposedly an "acquired taste." Real fans like them simply steamed and lightly covered with melted butter. They are more palatable to the uninitiated if they are served topped with a mild cheese sauce or mornay.

1 lb. small Brussels sprouts
2 tablespoons butter
2 tablespoons flour

1½ cups milk
½ cup heavy cream
½ cup grated Cheddar cheese
Salt and pepper to taste

Wash and trim loose leaves from sprouts and steam them in large saucepan until tender, usually 10 minutes. Drain and set aside, keeping warm. In small saucepan melt butter and slowly add flour, cooking over moderate heat for 3 minutes and stirring continually. Slowly add milk, stir well, and bring to a boil. Reduce heat and simmer for 10 minutes or until sauce begins to thicken. Add cream and stir, then add cheese and continue stirring until cheese melts. Add salt and white pepper to taste. Serve in small pitcher or pour over sprouts. Serves 4.

–Pumpkin Soup

I am rarely a fan of theater at the dinner table, but I once came away from a dinner party terribly impressed by a pumpkin soup that had been served from its shell. More than just a pretty gimmick, the shell still had enough pulp inside to thicken the delicious soup.

Try this soup served from one large tureen-size pumpkin in the center of the table or in individual small ones at each place.

4 small fresh pumpkins or 1 large
2 cups water
2 cups chicken stock
1 cup heavy cream
¼ teaspoon nutmeg
¼ teaspoon curry powder
½ teaspoon lemon juice
Chopped parsley

Remove seeds and pulp from pumpkins and place pumpkins in a long baking dish (or two if necessary) with enough water to cover bottom of pan(s). Steam in moderate oven for 10 minutes or until a spoon easily pries flesh from rind. Scrape flesh from pumpkins and put into large saucepan with water. Bring to a boil and simmer for 15 minutes, adding stock. Purée mixture in blender until smooth. Return to saucepan and add cream, nutmeg, and curry powder. Reheat and stir in lemon juice. Serve warm in pumpkin shells and garnish with chopped parsley. Serves 4.

–Pumpkin——————
Custard Pie

Pumpkin custard pie can be served either warm or cold. I like to make two or three at once.

4 eggs
1½ cups light cream
1 teaspoon vanilla
1½ cups steamed pumpkin
  or squash, well mashed
⅓ cup brown sugar
3 tablespoons molasses
½ teaspoon ginger
½ teaspoon cinnamon
⅛ teaspoon cloves
Pinch of salt
1 unbaked pie shell

Combine custard ingredients until smooth and pour into pie shell. Bake at 325° for 25 minutes or until barely firm. (Custard continues to cook as it cools.)

Cabbage

Cabbage is one of the few vegetables that appears in almost every cuisine throughout the world. Whether preserved as sauerkraut, shredded into slaw, or baked in an infinite number of ways, cabbage is delicious and well worth planting even in the smallest vegetable garden.

–Cabbage and——————
Swiss

1 small green cabbage, finely shredded
1 medium white onion, thinly sliced
¾ lb. Swiss cheese, grated
1 tablespoon caraway seeds
¾ teaspoon salt
½ cup bread crumbs
¾ cup milk

In Dutch oven, layer ⅓ of cabbage, then ⅓ of onion and cover with ⅓ of cheese. Sprinkle with 1 teaspoon of the caraway seeds and ¼ teaspoon of salt. Repeat layers twice and top with bread crumbs. Pour milk over top and bake at 350° for 25 minutes. Serves 8 as a side dish or 4 as a main course.

–Curried Cabbage

4 tablespoons olive oil
3 teaspoons curry powder
1 teaspoon garlic salt
Dash cayenne
1 small green cabbage, coarsely chopped
½ cup currants
⅓ cup sunflower seeds

Heat oil in large frying pan over medium heat. Add curry powder, garlic salt, and cayenne. After spices stop foaming, add cabbage and stir to coat with a light film of oil. Pour in ¼ cup water, cover tightly, and steam for 5 minutes or until cabbage is tender but crisp. Remove lid and add currants and sunflower seeds, tossing to mix. Replace lid and steam 5 minutes more. Serve hot. Serves 4.

–Sauerkraut

Sauerkraut is simple to prepare, but requires some attention to detail in order to be successful. Any variety of cabbage can be made into sauer-kraut, although the green ones are preferred. Whatever kind is used, good kraut demands fresh solid cabbage, a quantity of special pickling salt (which doesn't contain the additives of regular table salt), and a stoneware crock. A shredder is handy for cutting the slaw, but a sharp knife or cleaver used skillfully will do as well.

The major consideration in making sauerkraut is the temperature at which it is cured. If it is put in a place that never gets warmer than 60°, the re-sults will be firm, crisp, and evenly colored—all desirable characteristics of good kraut.

The cabbage should be packed firmly into the crock and covered com-pletely with brine. The top of the crock should be covered with a clean cloth and a plate. Place a weight on the plate to make the brine come close to the top of the crock and to wet the cloth. When fermentation begins, the muck from the top should be skimmed frequently and the cloth removed daily and thoroughly rinsed. Fermentation has ceased when no more bubbles rise to the top of the crock, which will happen in about a month if the proper temperature has been maintained.

The proportions of this brine should be precise—that is, 2 teaspoons of salt for 1 lb. of cabbage or ½ lb. of salt for 20 lbs. of cabbage.

PEARS

Although apples are the Northwest's biggest crop by volume, pears from Washington and Oregon are found on tables throughout the country. More than three thousand different varieties have been identified by botanists, and most of those have been grown in this country. Yet fewer than a dozen kinds of pears are of any commercial significance.

First in quantity, and some say in quality too, is the familiar Bartlett. On the market fresh from July into October, much of the Bartlett crop goes into cans, either by itself or blended into fruit cocktail.

Other well-known pears include Anjou, Bosc, and Comice, all of which thrive in the Pacific Northwest. Anjous are green-skinned, almost heart-shaped and sweet enough to eat fresh or use in cooking. Bosc pears are russet brown with a tapering neck and are best when used for cooking. The Comice variety is the picturebook fruit that is boxed in fancy gift assortments and shipped throughout the world. Peak season for all three is November through January, with Bosc appearing often in October and Anjou extending into April.

–Ginger Pears

Ginger pears are a fine accompaniment to meat, especially venison and other game. They also make a tasty sauce for ice cream.

4 small Bosc pears
½ cup water or pear juice
3 tablespoons brown sugar
1½ teaspoons crystallized ginger,
    chopped fine
1 tablespoon fresh mint leaves, crushed

Peel, core, and quarter pears. Pour water or juice into square baking pan; arrange pears with sugar, ginger, and mint sprinkled on top. Bake at 350° for 20 minutes or until fruit is soft. Serves 4.

–Fresh Pears and Cheese–

This simple pear salad should be a weekly feature when pears first arrive on local grocery shelves. Extra sharp Cheddar gives it especially good flavor.

3 large Comice pears, thoroughly ripened
12 red-leaf lettuce leaves,
   washed and patted dry
1 cup grated Cheddar cheese

–Dressing

½ cup olive oil
¼ cup cider vinegar
½ teaspoon garlic powder
½ teaspoon dill weed
1 teaspoon fresh oregano

Peel, halve, and core pears, arrange on lettuce leaves, and sprinkle with cheese. Put dressing ingredients in jar with tight-fitting lid and shake well. Pour over fruit. Serves 6.

–Poached Stuffed Pears–

Poached pears are among the most simple, but elegant, desserts in my repertoire. Both this version and the brandied one that follows are excellent.

6 Anjou pears, peeled, halved, and cored
2 cups water
1¼ cups honey
   ***or* 2 cups brown sugar**
1 teaspoon rum extract or almond extract
8 oz. cream cheese
¾ cup almonds, walnuts,
   or filberts, finely chopped

Boil water in large saucepan and add honey and extract, stirring until honey dissolves. Cook over high heat for 10 minutes. Reduce heat, place pear halves in liquid, and simmer for 10 minutes or until pears are soft. Remove pears and chill, reserving liquid in pan. Return liquid to high heat and reduce volume by half. Cream together cream cheese and nuts and stuff each pear half with this mixture. Ladle syrup over fruit and serve immediately. Serves 3–6.

–Brandied Pears

4 whole pears, peeled with stems left on
4 cups water
½ cup brandy
4 cloves
1 cinnamon stick
⅛ teaspoon nutmeg
3 lemon slices

Heat water, brandy, and spices in large saucepan to a rolling boil. Add whole pears and lemon slices. Reduce heat, and simmer for 8 minutes or until pears are soft. Cool and serve with crème fraîche or hard sauce. Serves 4.

–Fresh Pear Kuchen

Kuchen is a custardlike cake made with fresh fruit. Peaches may be used in place of the pears.

½ cup butter
2 cups whole-wheat flour
¼ teaspoon baking powder
½ teaspoon salt
¾ cup brown sugar

½ cup chopped walnuts
6 Bosc pears, halved
2 eggs, lightly beaten
1 cup light cream
½ teaspoon nutmeg
½ teaspoon cinnamon

Cut butter into small pieces and mix with flour, baking powder, salt, and 2 tablespoons of the sugar. Add nuts and press into bottom and halfway up sides of square baking pan. Arrange pear halves over nut mixture and sprinkle with cinnamon and remaining sugar. Bake at 400° for 15 minutes. Remove from oven and cover with mixture of eggs, nutmeg, and cream. Return to oven for 30 more minutes. Serve warm. Serves 8.

FILBERTS

Fall is the season for pear harvesting and also the time for gathering thousands of pounds of filberts or hazelnuts from groves in the Willamette Valley of Oregon. Almost all the filberts that are sold in this country are grown in this valley.

Filberts are expensive, fattening, and delightful tasting. A handful of them contains more calories than the equivalent amount of steak, sugar, or even chocolate cake. But these sweet round nuts are well worth the risk of gaining an extra pound or two.

Hazelnuts are a staple in Viennese, Swiss, and other central European desserts. The filberts that grow in Oregon, where they were first introduced over a hundred years ago, are related to the native European trees. The nuts grow in clusters on the branch and are covered with an open-ended husk, which conveniently releases the mature nut in the fall. The ground beneath the trees is swept to glean the nuts, which are then graded, dried, and shipped.

Like the European hazelnut, filberts are most often featured in elegant desserts and sweet snacks. They can be chopped and added to whole grains and fruit to make breakfast cereal, and they can also be used as the base for a sweet sauce for barbecued salmon.

–Filbert-Squash Soup

Filberts lend a fine flavor to this soup.

1½ cups cooked winter
    or acorn squash, mashed
1 cup filberts, finely chopped
½ cup onion, finely chopped
4 cups chicken stock
2 tablespoons butter
2 tablespoons dry sherry
¼ teaspoon pepper
Salt to taste

Combine squash, filberts, onion, and stock in large saucepan. Bring to a boil, cover, and simmer for 30 minutes, stirring occasionally. Add butter, sherry, pepper, and salt. Serves 4–6.

–Filbert-Chocolate Cream

This filbert cream dessert originally came from a Swedish cookbook and called for almonds instead of filberts. Since both nuts are very sweet and similar in flavor, I use them interchangeably in rich desserts.

4 egg whites
1⅓ cups sugar
1 cup filberts, finely ground
2½ cups whipping cream
1 tablespoon cornstarch
2 tablespoons cocoa

Beat egg whites until stiff, while adding 1 cup sugar by tablespoons. Grind filberts very fine in blender and fold into beaten egg whites. Pour into greased square baking pan and bake at 325° for 40 minutes or until firm.

Mix 1 cup whipping cream, remaining sugar, cornstarch, and cocoa together and cook in double boiler over high heat until cream thickens enough for stirring spoon to make a path. Cool and pour on top of nut meringue.

Whip remaining cream and spoon over chocolate cream. Dust lightly with cocoa. Serves 8.

PRESERVING THE HARVEST

It took me several vegetable gardens before I began planting with restraint in order to control the amount of harvested produce. There are still years when I have many more carrots, for instance, than I can possibly use, store, or give away in season. So then it is time to get out a big pot and a large colander and go to work, blanching and freezing the surplus.

Blanching, or heating briefly in boiling water, is important in order to make sure that the color, flavor, and texture of the vegetables remains intact after they have been frozen and thawed. The enzymes that promote growth will continue to work after the vegetable has been picked. Unless those enzymes are killed, the vegetables will rapidly deteriorate.

Blanching should only last for two or three minutes for most vegetables. They should then be removed quickly from the hot water, drained in a colander and rinsed with cold water until they are completely cool. Meal-size portions can then be ladled into clear plastic bags and sealed.

Tomatoes

Since most of my vegetables and fruits can be frozen, I rarely can them. Tomatoes are an exception, as canning is the only practical method of preservation. My mother's canning kettle gets a good workout for at least two or three days in the fall to insure a sufficient winter supply of home-grown tomatoes.

I dip whole firm tomatoes into boiling water for thirty seconds to loosen the skins and then peel them. I then pack the tomatoes to within an inch of the top of clean quart jars, add a teaspoon of salt to each, and seal the lids. Next the jars are placed in the canning kettle, covered with water, and left to boil for 45 minutes.

—Tomato Juice—

Another means of preserving tomatoes is to purée them into juice and freeze the juice in quart jars. The seasonings may vary; I sometimes add a dash of Worcestershire sauce or a handful of parsley.

3 large tomatoes, quartered
2 stalks celery, chopped
2 carrots, chopped
½ teaspoon fresh dill or oregano
½ teaspoon salt
1 teaspoon lemon juice

Purée in blender and serve chilled. Makes about 4 cups.

Pickles and Marmalade

Preservation of seasonal abundance also means pickles—from the dill and garlic varieties to relishes, chutneys, and conserves. And although the pickle barrel seems to have joined the ranks of the dodo, there are still a lot of cooks who make their own dill pickles, even if they don't preserve anything else.

The experts debate whether it is necessary to process a properly brined pickle in a boiling water bath before putting it onto the pantry shelf. I am a member of the more conservative school and do boil my pickle jars, secure in the knowledge that no one will get sick from my pickles since I go to all of that trouble. But my grandmother simply let her pickles ferment for several weeks, then moved them to clean jars, sealed the jars well—and no one ever suffered from eating her pickles!

Since the additives in table salt will darken cucumber dill pickles, only pickling salt should be employed for pickling. The water used should be free of additives and minerals if possible, and the vinegar should be of proper acidity (about 4 to 6 percent). Either distilled white vinegar or cider vinegar works well.

Pickling spices are packaged commercially—I usually use a locally blended brand. You can mix your own assortment if you like, using whole fresh spices such as allspice, clove, dill seed, mustard seed, nutmeg, ginger, and cayenne.

—Dill Pickles

3 dozen pickling cucumbers, 4 inches long
3 tablespoons pickling spice

12 heads of dill
1 pint vinegar
1½ cups pickling salt
8 quarts water

Wash and place cucumbers in large stone crock, covering with heads of dill and sprinkling with 2 tablespoons pickling spice. Mix 1 cup vinegar, ¾ cup salt, and 4 quarts water, and stir until salt dissolves. Pour over cucumbers and dill and set plate on top of vegetables to keep them covered with liquid. Store crock at 70° and let stand for 2 to 4 weeks, removing scum occasionally, until pickles are olive colored and well-flavored.

Sterilize quart jars and fill with pickles, pricking each pickle at both ends and once in the middle to prevent them from becoming hollow. Make new brine of 4 quarts water, ¾ cup salt, and 1 cup vinegar, and bring to a boil. Add remainder of pickling spice and pour brine into jars. Seal and process for 10 minutes in boiling water. Makes 6 quarts.

–Cucumber-Lime Marmalade

Pickling may be the time-honored method for preserving the summer's abundance of cucumbers, but I'm in love with this unusual marmalade.

2 cups cucumbers, finely chopped
4 cups sugar
⅓ cup fresh lime juice
   (requires approximately 3 limes)
2 tablespoons lime peel, grated
3 ounces liquid fruit pectin

Place cucumbers in large saucepan and add sugar, lime juice, and peel, stirring well. Bring to a rolling boil over high heat and allow to boil for exactly one minute, stirring constantly. Remove from heat and immediately stir in pectin. Skim foam, then stir and skim repeatedly for 5 minutes to eliminate floating particles.

Pack in pint jars and seal, leaving an inch of head room. Seal and process for 10 minutes in boiling water. Makes 2 pints.

–Dill Chunks

This simple way to preserve cucumbers also works well with zucchini.

3 medium cucumbers, cut into chunks
2 medium onions, sliced
2 celery stalks, cut into pieces
8 heads fresh dill
4 cups white distilled vinegar
4 cups sugar
½ cup pickling salt
1 tablespoon mustard seeds

Fill jars with cucumber chunks, alternating with onion slices, celery pieces, and heads of dill. Boil water and vinegar, add sugar, salt, and mustard seeds, and stir until dissolved. Pour liquid over cucumbers and seal jars. Process for 20 minutes in boiling water. Makes 4 quarts.

The Kitsap Peninsula, to the west of Seattle, used to be the center of a large dairy industry made up mostly of small farms settled by pioneers of Scandinavian descent. Milk, butter, and cheese were produced by almost every farmer. Some was sold locally, but most was sent into Seattle by small steamers.

Today, of course, many of those farms have been broken into even smaller parcels. Some still support livestock, but many have been sold to developers whose only produce is tract houses. Those farmers who are still in the dairy business are mostly members of a large multicounty cooperative that buys their milk in bulk and processes and sells dairy products all over the state.

The days of the independent farmer are over in Kitsap County, except for a few ambitious souls who keep their own small herds and sell milk almost exclusively to their neighbors. One such farmer, from whom I purchase fresh raw milk every week, boasts nine beautiful Jersey cows, and in her "spare" time maintains one of the finest gardens in the county. A remarkable woman, she gets up at five every morning to milk the cows and often doesn't end her day until nine or ten at night—after the last milk customer has returned home.

Her milk is sold in gallon pickle jars; its freshness and high quality is guaranteed by both the farmer and the county health department which corroborates her good intentions with weekly inspections.

Depending on the time of year and what the cows are eating, each gallon of milk is topped by three to six inches of cream. As if the freshness of the milk and quantity of cream were not enough, her prices are 30 percent below that of the local supermarkets.

Almost as famous as the farm's milk is the following zucchini relish, which is made in great quantity and often given away to numerous friends and family—and even to a favorite milk customer or two.

–Zucchini Relish

10 cups zucchini, peeled and ground
4 cups onions, ground
5 tablespoons pickling salt
2¼ cups white vinegar
4½ cups sugar
1 tablespoon mustard
1 tablespoon nutmeg
1½ teaspoons tumeric
1 tablespoon celery seed
½ teaspoon black pepper
1 green bell pepper, finely chopped
1 red bell pepper, finely chopped

Grind zucchini and onions in food mill. Stir together with pickling salt and let stand overnight. Rinse mixture and drain thoroughly. Place vinegar, sugar, and spices in large pot, and bring to a boil. Reduce heat and stir until sugar dissolves. Add vegetables, including peppers. Simmer over moderate heat for 30 minutes. Pack into clean quart jars and process for 10 minutes in boiling water bath. Makes 5–6 quarts.

WINTER

There is no such thing as a long winter's nap for most of us in the Pacific Northwest, who regard the weeks between Thanksgiving and early March as a season of high activity. Temperatures in Puget Sound and environs rarely drop below freezing, and outdoor activity continues nearly uninterrupted for most, whether they are runners, cyclists, or even gardeners. And some find themselves out of doors even more than ever when skiing season— both cross-country and downhill—begins.

It is a spectacular time of year to roam through the mountain forests, which are more beautiful than ever when covered with a thick blanket of snow. The rivers seem to freeze in motion and the fairylands of ice that result are magnificent. A few birds still in residence search eagerly for food as do the wary deer whose tracks occasionally break the snow. The air is crisp and clean and the silence dramatic. It is a wonderful season to be outdoors, especially if en route to a cozy fire in a rustic cabin for a weekend of relaxation.

The Olympic Mountains, and especially the Cascades, are both full of such idyllic retreats, built primarily for use in warmer months. Some friends and I often head out to one place that is perfect for four weekenders and is usually accessible after Christmas only on skis or snowshoes. With bunks in one corner and a table and kitchen sink in the other, the cabin is spartan, but comfortable. But it is the massive stone fireplace in the middle of the main room that makes this hideaway particularly inviting.

The main highway from Seattle to the Cascades is an efficient, impersonal interstate road, designed to transport thousands of cars and buses to crowded ski areas in the winter. Once the ski slopes are left behind, the traveler can easily get closer to the countryside by leaving the main road and heading down any one of the many logging roads in the area. These gravel roads are used commercially during the summer, but are closed in the late fall by the snow. One day last winter we left our car at the start of one of these roads, a ninety-minute trek from our destination. We each carried a share of the weekend food supply so our packs were quite light. Since there would be wood on hand at the cabin there was no need to carry any extra along. Skis were put on quickly and one behind the other we started down the road. The activity warmed us rapidly and at the first rest stop everybody took off one layer of clothing.

The road followed a small river, whose rapids were framed with icicles, some easily broken but others too solid to move. The quiet of the forest was precious—broken only by the rhythmic sound of our skis and the occasional rushing of water. There was little conversation as we glided down the road.

After several miles of gentle ups and downs, the road assumed a fairly steep upward grade for the last few hundred yards. With a few side steps the climb was over and the cabin appeared. Snow had drifted against the front door and had covered the woodpile in the back. But once inside, we lit kerosene lanterns and it wasn't too long before a fire was blazing, the room had warmed, and some wine was on the stove to mull. It promised to be a fine weekend away from the busy city.

Recreational activity is not the only winter outdoor pursuit in the Pacific Northwest. For this is the time that many commercial fishermen have their best seasons—especially those who harvest prawns, oysters, and Dungeness crab. Sport-fishing enthusiasts, too, are busy in the winter, because where the rivers are not frozen, steelhead trout—considered the best sport fishing in the region—are heading upriver to spawn.

Winter is also a fine time in the kitchen, especially for baking bread. Then there is Christmas, which seems to inspire even the most reluctant cook to spend a day or two in the kitchen, eagerly preparing a variety of holiday treats.

DUNGENESS CRAB

Although Dungeness crab are caught commercially from Mexico to Alaska, we in the Northwest have a special fondness for this delicious resource, since it is named for a small town on the Olympic Peninsula where the crab were first harvested commercially. Today, much of the entire West

Coast crab catch is taken off the Washington seacoast during December, January, and February. Inland waters also provide crab for the commercial fishermen, especially around the Washington–British Columbia border.

Crabbing attracts many recreational enthusiasts. All that is required to catch crabs in most waters of Puget Sound is a crab pot and bait. Other ways to gather crabs include wading at low tide with a net or setting a line off a dock or jetty. Only males can be legally harvested and they must be at least 6¼ inches across the shell to be kept. Interestingly, few females exceed the 6-inch measure.

Live crabs are a grayish green color which turns bright red upon cooking. Most crabs are sold pre-cooked, but in season they are always fresh. In the late spring and summer, only frozen crabs are usually available.

Live crabs can and some say should be cleaned before cooking, which is a fairly simple procedure. But the traditional method is to drop live crabs into a pot of boiling water and cook them for 15 minutes, remove and cool them, and then worry about cleaning.

The distinctively delicate flavor of the Dungeness has been described as a cross between Maine lobster and Maryland blue crab. Regardless of such descriptions, it is certain that Dungeness crab has a superb flavor. It is excellent in omelets, cream sauces rolled into crepes, and in salads with various mayonnaise dressings (the most popular of these being crab Louis). But my favorite of the standard preparations is deviled crab, baked and served in scallop shells.

–Deviled Crab

3 tablespoons butter
2 tablespoons flour
½ cup milk
½ cup heavy cream
1 teaspoon salt
¼ teaspoon nutmeg
Dash dry hot mustard
¼ cup dry sherry
¼ teaspoon fresh lemon juice
1 teaspoon Worcestershire sauce
2 egg yolks, lightly beaten
2 cups fresh crabmeat
Bread crumbs
Lemon wedges

In large frying pan melt butter and add flour, stirring constantly for several minutes over low heat. In small saucepan bring milk and cream to a boil and add to butter and flour, stirring vigorously until sauce is smooth. Remove from heat and stir in salt and spices, sherry, lemon juice, and Worcestershire sauce. Add egg yolks and crabmeat, return mixture to heat, and cook for 3 minutes. Pour into scallop shells or other ramekins and cover with bread crumbs. Bake at 425° for 15 minutes or until brown, and serve accompanied with lemon wedges. Serves 4.

–Crab Baked with–
Almonds and Cheese

This variation of crab au gratin comes from a kitchen regularly supplied with fresh crab from a pot set out just beyond the beach in front of the house.

1 small green pepper, chopped
¼ cup butter
4 teaspoons arrowroot
1 cup evaporated milk
⅓ cup water
½ teaspoon salt
½ teaspoon chervil
1 cup sliced celery
2 tablespoons chopped pimiento
1 lb. fresh crabmeat
2 hardboiled eggs, coarsely chopped
½ cup buttered bread crumbs
½ cup shredded Cheddar cheese
½ cup toasted slivered almonds

Sauté green pepper in butter melted in large frying pan. Remove from heat
and stir in arrowroot. Combine evaporated milk with water. Add to butter,
green pepper, and arrowroot. Return all to low heat and cook slowly, stirring constantly until sauce is thick and smooth. Stir in salt, chervil, celery,
pimiento, and crabmeat. Add eggs. Pour into greased long baking pan. Top
with buttered crumbs, shredded cheese, and almonds. Bake at 350° for 30
minutes. Serves 3–4.

–Crab Cioppino

*Cioppino seems almost as common as apple pie in parts of the Northwest.
It can feature a variety of seafood or just one particular favorite. The
tomato-based sauce will enhance whatever is finally put into the pot. The
sauce should be allowed to simmer slowly for several hours before the seafood is added.*

*Beginners are advised to eat cioppino with very large napkins in hand.
These napkins can double as bibs when necessary.*

> **2 large cloves garlic**
> **3 tablespoons olive oil**
> **2 cups stewed tomatoes**
> **2 cups tomato sauce**
> **1 medium onion, sliced**
> **1 teaspoon sugar**
> **1 teaspoon Tabasco sauce**
> **½ cup white wine**
> **2 cups water**
> **1 celery stalk, chopped**
> **¼ cup parsley, chopped**
> **Salt**
> **Freshly ground black pepper**
> **12 butter clams**
> **2 whole crabs, cleaned and cracked**

In large Dutch oven or stockpot sauté garlic in olive oil until tender. Add
tomatoes, tomato sauce, sugar, Tabasco, wine, and water, and simmer
over medium heat for 10 minutes. Add celery, parsley, and onion, salt and
pepper and reduce heat to low. Simmer for at least 1 hour. Add clams and
crab. Increase to medium heat and cover for 10 minutes, stirring occasionally, or until clams open. Serves 5–6.

–Crab-Stuffed Won Tons

My favorite local restaurant features seasonal specialties, cooked and served in a variety of unusually delicious ways. Dungeness crab is a mainstay of the menu in the winter; these hors d'oeuvres are pure genius.

12 oz. package frozen won ton skins

—Filling

**1 lb. spinach
1 cup water chestnuts, finely chopped
Crabmeat from 1 whole cooked crab, shredded
½ bunch scallions, chopped, including tops
1 tablespoon dry sherry
1 tablespoon soy sauce
1 tablespoon grated fresh ginger
2 tablespoons cornstarch
3 cups vegetable stock or chicken stock**

Thaw won ton skins. In large saucepan wilt spinach very slightly, drain, then cool and chop. Combine spinach with remaining filling ingredients, and let this mixture rest for 20 minutes. Carefully separate squares of won ton. Put a teaspoonful of filling in center of each, wet edge with finger, and place another skin on top, and press with finger to seal. Place stuffed won tons on a baking sheet dusted with cornstarch until ready to cook.

Bring vegetable, or chicken stock to a rolling boil in Dutch oven. Boil stuffed won tons 5 to 8 minutes. Serves 4.

PRAWNS AND SHRIMP

Prawns and shrimp are caught commercially along the Washington-Oregon seacoasts and in the large deep inlets of British Columbia and Vancouver Island, as well as off the San Juan Islands, in Hood Canal, and in Puget Sound. Among experts the terms shrimp and prawn seem to be fairly interchangeable, although prawn is usually reserved for the larger varieties. These shellfish customarily live at depths of 180 to 300 feet and are best when harvested from October through May. Since they are most easily harvested with special equipment, prawns are most often fished commercially, although recreationists do set traps from time to time.

Most ocean shrimp are caught with a trawl, while the inland varieties are trapped in wire-mesh pots. The typical prawn fisherman sets some two hundred to three hundred traps each season and twice a day goes from one to the next pulling them to the surface with a mechanical winch. Spot prawns, such as those caught in Alberni Inlet on Vancouver Island, are among the largest found in the Northwest and may average only ten to the pound. Ocean shrimp and those from Washington's Hood Canal often average as many as ninety to the pound.

Prawns and shrimp, whether fresh or frozen, must be carefully prepared, as their delicate flesh cooks very quickly and becomes mushy if overcooked. When prawns are available fresh, it is best to steam them whole, then separate the head from the body and remove the shell. Unlike most shrimp, Northwest prawns have no sand vein, which makes them much easier to clean.

As a rule three to five minutes in boiling water should be allowed if the shrimp are small and six to eight minutes if they are large. Many people prefer to eat prawns prepared as simply as possible. They are superb just steamed, chilled, and served with an interesting sauce or two.

–Shrimp Dip

This dip is fine for crab too.

2 eggs
½ teaspoon salt
2 teaspoons dry mustard
1 teaspoon honey
4 tablespoons lemon juice
¾ cup olive oil
1 tablespoon minced parsley
1 tablespoon minced scallions
½ teaspoon horseradish
½ teaspoon freshly ground pepper
Dash cayenne
½ teaspoon fresh tarragon, chopped

In a blender combine eggs, salt, mustard, honey, and lemon juice, and whirl until well blended. Drizzle in oil while blending at medium-high speed until mixture begins to thicken. Transfer to a bowl, add remaining ingredients, and blend thoroughly. Makes 1 cup.

–Prawn Sauté

This simple prawn sauté is an elegant main dish. It should be served with long-grain or brown rice.

4 tablespoons butter
¼ cup dry sherry
⅛ teaspoon powdered ginger
1 medium clove garlic, mashed
32 medium prawns, peeled and cleaned
Juice of ½ lemon

In large saucepan melt butter and allow it to brown lightly. Add sherry, ginger, and garlic. Stir and simmer for 2 minutes, then add prawns. Simmer over medium heat for 4 minutes more, then sprinkle with lemon juice. Stir twice and remove from heat. Serves 4.

–Riddled Shrimp

This recipe for riddled shrimp comes from an island off the coast of South Carolina where shrimp are harvested nearly year round. I know of one kitchen there where a pot of shrimp is always marinating in the refrigerator, especially in the summer when houseguests are many—and hungry. Riddled shrimp can be served on sandwiches, in salads, or as an hors d'oeuvre, impaled on toothpicks with pieces of orange or lemon.

9 lbs. shrimp, cleaned and cooked
2 large onions, sliced in rings
2 large green peppers, sliced in rings
4 cups apple cider vinegar
1 cup olive oil
2 cups ketchup
2 tablespoons freshly ground black pepper
1 clove garlic, mashed
1 oz. pickling spice
1 teaspoon allspice
4 bay leaves
1 teaspoon coriander seeds

In stoneware crock, place layers of shrimp, then onion, then pepper until all are used. Stir cider vinegar and oil together until thoroughly blended. Add ketchup, garlic, and spices to vinegar mixture and stir. Pour this sauce over shrimp and let stand in refrigerator for 2 weeks. Makes 30 servings.

–Barbecued Prawns–

A quick marinade for prawns uses soy sauce and garlic. The marinated prawns can be put on skewers and broiled over charcoal for 2 or 3 minutes. The skewers can also hold pineapple chunks, tomatoes, green peppers, onions, water chestnuts, or mushrooms. The important thing is not to overcook the prawns.

> **½ cup olive oil**
> **¼ cup soy sauce**
> **1 medium clove garlic, mashed**
> **4 whole allspice**
> **Dash cayenne**
> **1 lb. prawns, peeled and cleaned**

Blend oil, soy sauce, garlic, allspice, and cayenne together until well mixed. Spoon this marinade over prawns and let stand for 2 hours. Drain and put on skewers with assorted vegetables and fruit. Grill briefly over hot charcoal and serve. Serves 3–4.

–Jambalaya Alberni–

This jambalaya was born one weekend after a local prawn fisherman came home to my neighborhood with an entire day's catch. We had several rounds of omelets, crepes, and soufflés, and on the final night decided to do something special. Rex's Crab Boil is an excellent commercial shrimp and crab seasoning that combines mustard, dill, and coriander seed, red and black pepper, laurel and thyme leaves, allspice and cloves.

> 4 cups water
> 1 oz. Rex's Crab Boil
> 24 large prawns
> 2 cups rice
> 1 large shallot, minced
> 1 small onion, chopped
> ¼ lb. ham, cubed
> 1 package frozen or 1½ cups fresh peas
> 2 small tomatoes, chopped
> 1 bunch scallions, chopped
> ½ lb. mushrooms, sliced
> 1 small can tomato sauce
> ¼ cup olive oil
> ½ teaspoon cayenne pepper
> 1 teaspoon salt
> ½ teaspoon freshly ground black pepper
> 2 tablespoons capers

Bring water to a boil in large Dutch oven and add Rex's Crab Boil and prawns (with heads and tails intact). Boil for 3 minutes if fresh or for 6 if frozen. Remove prawns (reserving cooking water), and immediately place them in cold water for several minutes to stop cooking and then drain. Return cooking water to a boil. Add rice and steam until all water is absorbed, but rice is still quite moist—about 20 minutes. While rice is cooking, clean the prawns, by peeling them and removing the heads.

Add shallot, onion, and ham to rice. If frozen peas are being used, add them at this point. Combine tomato sauce, olive oil, cayenne, salt, and pepper, and mix well. Pour over rice, cover pot, and bake at 350° for 15 minutes.

Remove rice from oven and add mushrooms, peas (if fresh), tomatoes, scallions, capers, and prawns. Stir and return to oven for 10 minutes or until vegetables are tender. Serves 6.

–Shrimp Creole

Here's the Northwest version of a great Southern favorite.

3 tablespoons butter
1 medium onion, chopped
2 cloves garlic, mashed
3 tablespoons flour
3 stalks celery, chopped
½ lb. sliced mushrooms
1 green pepper, chopped
1½ tablespoons salt
1 teaspoon thyme
½ bay leaf
¼ teaspoon cayenne
½ teaspoon Tabasco sauce
¼ cup dry white wine
1 lb. raw cleaned shrimp
1 lemon, halved

Melt butter in large frying pan and sauté onion, garlic, and celery. Add flour and remaining ingredients, except shrimp and lemon. Keep sauce warm. Meanwhile, cook shrimp with lemon in 1 quart boiling water in Dutch oven for 3 minutes. Drain shrimp, add them to sauce, and simmer for 10 minutes. Serve over rice. Serves 4.

OYSTERS

Nothing is more typical of the abundance of the Pacific Northwest—or as incomparably delicious—as the famous Olympia oysters. These marvelous creatures, which sometimes number as many as two thousand to a gallon jar, are prized by gourmets for their delicacy and flavor. The successful growth of the Olympia oyster inspired the importation of larger Japanese varieties to Puget Sound waters at the turn of the century. Many commercial farms in business today have their roots in that pioneer enterprise.

Currently the annual harvest of oysters in Washington alone is valued at ten million dollars and accounts for nearly 10 percent of the national total. Willapa Bay in southwestern Washington and Hood Canal on the eastern edge of the Olympic Peninsula are the principal locations for the commercial operations, since in those waters there are ideal conditions for oyster cultivation. These areas also support a number of privately seeded oyster beds which are maintained by and for local residents. But there are also a few public tidelands, especially on Hood Canal, where tourists can stop and shuck a bushel or two.

Although the natural plenitude of oysters in Washington has notably decreased as oystermen and recreationists carefully monitor the local crop, parts of Vancouver Island in British Columbia still have oysters in great numbers which can be gathered by residents and tourists alike. These are also Pacific oysters, brought originally to the region by Japanese cannery workers and loggers who came to the island early in the century. Their legacy has sustained itself remarkably in a number of bays and inlets all around Vancouver Island.

Cortez Island, a small, sparsely populated place located several miles from the main island and several hundred miles up the coast from Victoria, is one such community that thrives on oysters. I spent a Christmas weekend on Cortez one year and was sent out for oysters early in the visit. Rarely had I seen such great numbers of oysters and certainly not in beds that were legally open for recreational picking.

Although the strictest of oyster connoisseurs insist that the best way to consume their passion is on the half shell, I have a special fondness for oyster stew, especially as it was prepared on Christmas Eve on Cortez that year. The oysters were just minutes from the water, and the cream and milk had been collected from a neighbor's cow that morning. Surely there was never a more memorable—or fresher—oyster stew.

–Northwest Oyster Stew–

1 pint (or 18) fresh oysters
1 cup heavy cream
3 cups milk
1 teaspoon salt
1 tablespoon Worcestershire sauce
Cayenne to taste
2 tablespoons butter
Chopped parsley

Shuck oysters if necessary, reserving liquor. In large Dutch oven, simmer oysters in liquor over low heat for about 3 minutes or until edges begin to curl. Add cream and milk, and heat until bubbles form around edge of pot, but not until boiling. Then add salt, Worcestershire, and cayenne in pinches to taste. Remove from heat and add butter. Garnish with chopped parsley. Serves 4.

–Cortez Oysters–

Cortez natives could fill several cookbooks with tasty oyster recipes. These deviled oysters top the list.

2 tablespoons butter
2 tablespoons flour
1 cup light cream
¼ teaspoon salt
⅛ teaspoon white pepper
½ teaspoon dill
Dash nutmeg
18 oysters in shell
4 strips bacon, cooked and crumbled
1½ cups grated Cheddar or Monterey jack cheese

Melt butter in small saucepan and add flour, cooking for several minutes over low heat and stirring constantly. Remove from heat and add cream, salt, and pepper, and stir until smooth. Return to medium heat and stir until thick. Add dill and nutmeg and set aside.

Shuck oysters, reserving lower shells. Cut oysters into small pieces or put through a food mill. Put 2 tablespoons sauce into each shell and fill with ground oysters. Top with bacon bits and grated cheese. Place under hot broiler for 4 minutes or until cheese melts. Serves 4.

–Oysters and Bleu Cheese

A simple sauce and basic seasoning seem to bring out the best in a bucket of oysters, especially for those who prefer a slight disguise. Fresh oysters should be used if available and they should be shucked over a pot to retain as much liquor as possible.

3 tablespoons butter
3 tablespoons flour
¾ cup dry white wine
¼ lb. bleu cheese, crumbled into small pieces
18 to 24 fresh oysters

In medium frying pan melt butter and add flour, cooking for several minutes over low heat and stirring constantly. Add wine and any liquor from oysters and stir until smooth. Then add bleu cheese and simmer until cheese is completely melted and sauce is smooth.

Increase heat to medium and add oysters to sauce. Let oysters poach lightly by simmering for 5 minutes, stirring constantly. Serve hot on steamed rice. Serves 4.

–Oysters in Brown Sauce

2 tablespoons butter
2 tablespoons flour
1 tablespoon soy sauce
1 cup oyster liquor
1 pint oysters or 18 in shell
Salt and pepper to taste

In medium frying pan melt butter and add flour, cooking for several minutes over low heat and stirring continually. Add soy sauce and liquor from oysters and stir until smooth. Add oysters and simmer for 3 minutes. Serve warm over rice. Serves 4.

–Oyster Fritters––––––––––

Oyster fritters should be eaten with the fingers and can be dipped into small bowls of applesauce, soy sauce, sour cream, or yogurt.

> **1 cup flour**
> **1 teaspoon baking powder**
> **½ teaspoon salt**
> **1 egg, lightly beaten**
> **⅔ cup milk**
> **1 cup cooked corn, fresh if possible**
> **½ cup parsley, chopped**
> **½ cup onions, finely chopped**
> **2 cups oysters, drained and chopped**
> **Cooking oil for deep-frying**

Mix flour, baking powder, and salt together. Add egg and milk and stir until smooth. Add vegetables and oysters and blend until thoroughly mixed. Drop by tablespoons into hot fat in deep pot and let cook for 3 minutes or until golden. Serves 6.

–Hangtown Fry––––––––––

The Hangtown Fry was supposedly invented during the California Gold Rush days and is said to have been the village specialty of a place known as Hangtown which was later renamed Placerville by its image-conscious citizens. This oyster-and-egg combination is a standard on many Northwest restaurant menus and makes a fine luncheon or supper dish.

The oysters should be dusted in flour and browned in butter before adding the beaten eggs to the pan. Try sprinkling freshly grated Parmesan cheese over the finished product.

> **6 small to medium oysters**
> **4 tablespoons butter**
> **Flour**
> **6 eggs, well beaten**
> **3 tablespoons cream**
> **½ teaspoon salt**
> **¼ cup chopped parsley**

Dust oysters in flour and fry until golden in melted butter in medium frying pan. Blend together eggs, cream, salt and parsley, and pour over oysters. Reduce heat to low and cover. Serve when eggs are set. Serves 2–3.

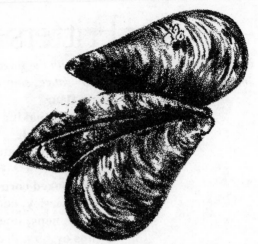

MUSSELS

Mussels have recently become a "find" on trendy tables around the Northwest, as well as in other coastal regions of America. Yet these tasty little mollusks have been a mainstay of seafood cuisine in Europe for centuries, where they are even cultivated in great numbers with success. Blue mussels are extremely plentiful in the Northwest, since all that they need to thrive are favorable tidal conditions and a rock on which to grow.

Although they are somewhat soft in the summer (their spawning season), mussels from Puget Sound are edible throughout the year. Like most other shellfish, the best season for mussels seems to be winter, or maybe that is when I feel most inspired to walk down to the beach and gather them. A sharp knife and an empty bucket is all the necessary equipment. It takes me less than fifteen minutes to harvest enough for an entire meal.

Although mussels may be carriers of the paralytic shellfish poisoning that sometimes comes from red tide, such danger is confined in the Pacific Northwest to mussels from areas of open ocean or high salinity. The inland waters are perfectly safe from this problem. Several other types of red tide, which is caused by masses of single-celled animals, do occasionally occur in Puget Sound, but none has ever been known to be dangerous.

Cleaning the mussels is important: it is a simple matter of scrubbing each one with a stiff brush and pulling or cutting away the "beard" or byssus from the shell. Unlike clams, mussels are usually quite clean inside their tightly closed shells, so they may be steamed open as soon as their exterior has been scrubbed.

I have collected mussels at the ocean in the fall and winter and simply steamed them and used garlic butter for a dip. They are a common addition to any seafood stew or chowder, but can be cooked alone in many different ways.

–Mussels Marinière–

Mussels marinière is a classic, simple and wonderful with a tartly dressed green salad and lots of homemade sourdough French bread.

> **4 dozen mussels, cleaned**
> **4 leeks, chopped**
> **½ cup parsley, chopped**
> **4 garlic cloves, minced**
> **1¼ cups white wine**
> **Freshly ground black pepper**

Place mussels in large Dutch oven or stockpot and add leeks, parsley, and garlic. Pour in wine, cover, and steam about 5 minutes or until mussels open. Remove meat from shells, strain liquid, and add pepper to taste. Return mussels to liquid and serve. Serves 3–4.

–Sweet-Cooked– Mussels

This Japanese-style treatment sweetens the mussels nicely and makes a delicious hor d' oeuvre.

> **½ cup sake**
> **1 tablespoon honey**
> **¼ cup soy sauce**
> **1 teaspoon grated fresh ginger**
> **3 dozen mussels, steamed and shucked**
> **1 tablespoon cornstarch**

Combine sake, honey, soy, and ginger in large frying pan and bring to a boil. Add mussels and cook over medium heat for 3 minutes. Remove mussels from liquid and add cornstarch, mixing thoroughly. Bring to a boil and cook until thickened, stirring continually. Return mussels to sauce and coat evenly. Serves 12 as hors d'oeuvre.

–Mussels Gratinée————

A gratinée is another good hors d' oeuvre or appetizer.

3 tablespoons tomato paste
2 tablespoons olive oil
1 small garlic clove, mashed
3 dozen mussels, steamed and
  removed from shells, reserving half of shells
1 cup freshly grated Parmesan cheese

Combine tomato paste, oil, and garlic until smooth. Place each mussel in single reserved shell on baking sheet and cover with a dab of tomato mixture. Sprinkle cheese over top of each mussel and place under hot broiler for 3 minutes or until cheese melts and browns. Serves 12.

SQUID AND OCTOPUS

Even those in the Pacific Northwest who are extremely dedicated to living with natural abundance rarely encounter the wonderful delicacy of squid. Exalted in Japanese cuisine, these "exotic" creatures—which are unusually flavorful and nutritious—have been all but overlooked by Americans.

Squid come from cold waters in the Strait of Juan de Fuca and farther north. Although they occasionally come to the surface in fishing nets, squid are generally caught by scuba divers. Like their cousins the octopi, squid can propel themselves rapidly and will squirt their ink to darken the water as soon as they sense danger.

–Savory Squid————

There are many ways to prepare squid. A friend of mine who dives and brings home squid prepares it this way.

3 lbs. squid
3 teaspoons olive oil
1 medium onion, sliced
3 garlic cloves, minced
2 cups whole tomatoes, cut into chunks

½ cup tomato paste
¼ cup red wine
2 tablespoons fresh basil, minced
1 teaspoon salt
1 teaspoon fresh oregano

Slit whole squid with scissors and remove mouth, eyes, innards, and inside shell. Cut body and tentacles into 3 or 4 pieces. In large frying pan heat olive oil and sauté onion and garlic. Then add squid and gently sauté over low heat until lightly browned. Add tomatoes, tomato paste, wine, basil, salt, and oregano, and simmer for 30 to 45 minutes. Serve over rice topped with grated Parmesan cheese. Serves 4.

The large octopus is very common in Puget Sound. It is usually found at depths of thirty to sixty feet and is very difficult to catch. It is illegal to spear or mutilate the octopus in any way, so to net one, it must be surprised and forced to the surface before it can attach its powerful suckers to a convenient rock.

Octopi are delicious in a succulent way, although the meat is often very chewy. Since they live exclusively on clams and crabs, it is easy to understand why their meat tastes so good!

Cleaning an octopus is simply a matter of turning the head inside out and cutting the few muscles that hold the viscera in place. Once the innards are removed, the beak and ink sacs should be cut away. The meat (both head and tentacles) should then be rubbed with rock salt to remove the animal's protective slime, then well rinsed, and it will be ready for the pot.

Lightly pounding the meat will tenderize it. Raw octopus is excellent when sliced very thin and dipped into bowls of soy sauce and vinegar. It can also be sautéed in melted butter and garlic until lightly browned and then served with rice. Octopus can also be boiled (the most common Japanese method of preparation), in four quarts of water with four teaspoons of soy sauce, after the tentacles and head have been cut into pieces 1-inch thick. The meat should be boiled for 5 minutes, or longer if the meat is cut any thicker.

ABALONE AND SCALLOPS

Much more in demand than either squid or octopus, but fairly scarce in Washington waters, is the abalone. Since the population is so small there is no commercial harvest of this seafood, as there is in California. But local divers seek them actively and can often net the daily limit of five, especially if searching near the rock shorelines of the San Juan Islands.

Abalone attach themselves to rocks, especially to those that are covered with seaweed and so serve as good camouflage. They usually can be found twenty-five to forty feet below the low-tide mark. The gatherer must be calm and quiet, as any excitement will cause the abalone to cling desparately—and immovably—to his rock. Divers use a special abalone iron to pry these mollusks free.

Purple-hinged scallops also inhabit the same San Juan Island areas. Like abalone, these scallops cling to rocks and are sufficiently scarce to attract only recreationists.

Either abalone or scallops can be sautéed in a savory butter to enhance their delicate flavor. Abalone should be pounded for several seconds and sliced into strips. Scallops can be eaten whole or cut into pieces, depending upon their size.

–Seafood Simmer

4 tablespoons butter
¼ cup sweet white wine
1 tablespoon shallots, finely chopped
1 tablespoon parsley, finely chopped
2 large abalone
2 large scallops

In medium frying pan melt butter and add wine. When bubbling add shallots and parsley and cook over moderate heat for 2 minutes. Then add shellfish and cook for 5 minutes, stirring occasionally. Serves 3–4.

STEELHEAD TROUT

Winter temperatures may discourage the casual recreational fisherman. But nothing deters the trophy hunter in search of steelhead trout, whose season as at its peak during December and January. It takes patience, experience, and a great deal of luck to land even one steelhead every season.

Considered the prime trophy fish of the Pacific Northwest, steelhead annually challenge over two hundred thousand eager anglers.

Although winter steelhead are the most popular, the fish can actually be caught in Washington during other months of the year as well. A rainbow trout that spends its life heading out to the ocean and returning to spawn two years later, the average steelhead weighs eight pounds, but many frequently weigh in at twenty pounds. Unlike salmon, steelhead spawn several times during a lifetime. Small numbers of steelhead trout are harvested commercially by local Indian tribes, but most of the ones that end up on Northwest tables are caught by sport fishermen. Steelhead provide great sport for even the most seasoned anglers. They are generally caught in rugged rivers and streams—the more rugged the area the more likely a catch. Fishermen in wading gear often wait for the fish while standing in waist-high water or balancing precariously in small boats. Steelhead tackle is somewhat lighter than salmon gear and is also slightly longer and more sensitive. Every fisherman has a favorite lure or fly, but no one claims to have discovered one that always works. Steelhead are just too unpredictable to make things that easy.

Steelhead is frequently likened to salmon because of its firm meaty texture, and it is usually prepared in a similar manner. Poaching is a suitable cooking method for an average steelhead, and the larger ones can also be cut into steaks or fillets.

–Irish Fish Company–
Pan-Fried Steelhead

This very basic recipe came from the days before refrigeration, when lemon juice was used to keep fish from spoiling, rather than simply to enhance its flavor. Fish prepared according to this recipe may be cooked either on top of the stove or over a campfire.

> **4 steelhead steaks, ½–¾ inches thick**
> **Lemon pepper**
> **1 tablespoon butter**
> **1 tablespoon olive oil**
> **½ cup butter**
> **Juice of ½ lemon**
> **Few sprigs parsley, coarsely chopped**

Sprinkle steaks generously with lemon pepper and sauté in large frying pan over moderate heat in butter and olive oil for about 15 minutes or until lightly browned. Turn and cook another 10 minutes or until second side is brown. In medium saucepan, melt butter and stir in lemon juice. Toss in parsley, mix well, and pour over steaks. Serves 4.

–Baked Steelhead Trout–

Steelhead trout has a delicate flavor which far surpasses even the most tasty king salmon. It is more than qualified to take the place of the Christmas turkey or to serve as the centerpiece for other celebratory feasts. I treat my friends to baked steelhead at least once during the winter holiday season.

8–10-lb. steelhead trout, cleaned
2 medium garlic cloves, mashed
½ teaspoon freshly ground black pepper
1 teaspoon ground thyme
½ teaspoon celery salt
½ cup butter
½ cup olive oil
3 tablespoons fresh lemon juice
1½ cups sour cream or crème fraîche
4 scallions, finely chopped
Parsley
1 lemon, cut into thin wedges

Fillet fish, leaving skin intact, and place fillets skin-side down in long baking pan. Spread garlic evenly on fillets and sprinkle with seasonings. Melt butter in medium saucepan and add oil and lemon juice. Stir well and baste each fillet thoroughly. Bake for 25 minutes at 300° or until fish is slightly flaky when touched with fork. Remove from oven and let cool for 10 minutes. Cover fillets with sour cream or crème fraîche and sprinkle with scallions. Return to oven and broil for 3 to 5 minutes, or until sour cream begins to bubble. Garnish with parsley sprigs and lemon wedges. Serves 8.

SOURDOUGH

Sourdough starters are said to have helped win the West, fill Fort Knox with gold from Alaska, and put San Francisco on the map. All such claims aside, it can certainly be said that without the natural leavening provided by an active sourdough starter, both pioneers and prospectors would have frequently gone hungry. Used in those days to make bread and pancakes and even an occasional dessert, the sourdough starter was a precious resource, passed along from friend to friend and from family to family.

Although today's sourdough cookery may not be so romantic, it is undoubtedly more ambitious. All sorts of breads, pancakes, and desserts have been perfected by sourdough enthusiasts, especially in the West. Many good kitchens in the Pacific Northwest maintain a sourdough starter and rely on it as a major source of homemade bread.

A sourdough starter is simply a home yeast factory, begun and perpetuated with flour and water, which is stored in a warm place until natural fermentation occurs. An active starter must be used and replenished weekly. So if a cup of starter is removed from the crock and mixed with flour and water to make a batter or dough, then a cup of that mixture should be returned to the starter before the rest of the recipe is completed.

Once the starter is alive and well, cold storage is required to keep it in good condition. A glass or stoneware crock with a tight-fitting lid is fine for this purpose (metal containers should not be used). If well fed and frequently used, the starter will last indefinitely, provided that nothing but flour and water ever goes into the crock.

There are many different methods of making a sourdough starter. Since mine came from a friend's own supply (the most reliable method of all), I hesitate to recommend any one way of beginning a starter over another. There are powdered commercial starters on the market, as well as a variety of ways to start from scratch. The most popular method is to combine 2 cups of white flour, 1 package of baker's yeast, and a little over 1 cup of water, to make a thick batter. Left in a warm, draft-free place, this yeast-assisted mixture will be bubbling nicely within 24 hours. Without the yeast, the same process takes four or five days to work.

Variations on the above methods include the substitution of milk for water, the use of water from boiled potatoes, or sometimes the addition of a bit of sugar. Contrary to some opinions, new starters work very well. It is not the age of the starter that is important—it is the activity in the crock that counts.

A few simple tricks make sourdough cookery practically foolproof. First, the starter should always be used and replenished at room temperature—if it is stored in the refrigerator, it should be taken out several hours before use. Second, once the dough is made, it should be kneaded quickly and with a minimum of strokes, as excessive handling permits the escape of the leavening gases produced by the yeast. Finally, it should be remembered that sourdough bread needs longer baking at a higher temperature than other yeast bread.

If you like the yeasty taste of sourdough, then you will probably want to try it in almost everything that you bake at home. I have seen recipes for such wonders as chocolate cake, English muffins, and doughnuts, all made with sourdough, and I have been assured that they are all delicious.

The two following bread recipes will give you the basics of sourdough baking at its best.

–Basic Sourdough–
Bread

1 cup sourdough starter from crock
2½ cups whole-wheat flour
2 cups warm water

Combine these ingredients, cover, and let ferment overnight in a warm place. Next morning, add 1 cup of fermented mixture to starter crock. Three cups will remain. These should be used to complete this recipe.

3 cups starter mixture
6½ cups whole-wheat
    or other whole-grain flour
2 tablespoons honey
2 teasooons salt
1½ cups milk
2 tablespoons melted butter

Combine starter, 3 cups of the flour, honey, salt, milk, and butter, and beat with wooden spoon for 200 strokes. Slowly add remainder of flour until dough is too stiff to stir. Turn out on floured board and knead, adding flour as needed, until dough is satiny smooth. Place in oiled bowl, turn once, and let rise in warm place until double in bulk. Punch down and let rise again until doubled. Form dough into two loaves and place in greased loaf pans. Let double in bulk once more and bake at 400° for 1 hour.

–Sourdough French Bread

Follow directions for making starter in Basic Sourdough Bread recipe.

3 cups starter mixture
7 cups unbleached white flour
2 teaspoons salt
¼ cup oil
3 tablespoons honey
½ cup milk
1 tablespoon corn meal

Combine all ingredients except 3 cups of the flour and the corn meal. Beat at least 200 strokes or until well blended (use dough hook on electric mixer if available). Let batter rest for 1 hour. Add remaining flour and knead it in carefully on floured board until dough is satiny smooth. Let dough double in bulk, punch it down, and divide it into 2 pieces. Roll out dough in rectangle on floured board to ¼-inch thickness. Roll up widthwise like a jelly-roll, sealing ends and pinching seam together. Rock each loaf on board to improve and even its shape. Place seam-side down on baking sheet sprinkled with corn meal. Let loaves rise until doubled, then slash the tops with a sharp knife. Place baking pan filled with water on lowest oven rack, and bake the loaves at 400° for 45 minutes, or until crusts are a rich brown.

–Sourdough Pretzels

These sourdough pretzels are a nice variation on the famous Philadelphia soft pretzels, sold by street vendors all over that town.
Follow directions for making starter in Basic Sourdough Bread recipe.

3 cups starter mixture
2 cups whole-wheat flour
2 cups white flour
2½ cups rye flour
¼ cup molasses
2 teaspoons salt
3 tablesooons oil
1 egg beaten with 2 tablespoons water
Sea salt or kosher salt

Combine starter, 1 cup whole-wheat flour, 1 cup white flour, rye flour, molasses, salt, and oil. Beat hard with wooden spoon for 200 strokes until well blended and let rest for 1 hour. Slowly add remaining flour, turn out dough onto floured board, and knead until satiny smooth. Let rise until double in bulk. Punch down, pinch off egg-size pieces, roll out ten inches long and twist into pretzel shape. Brush each pretzel with egg and invert in dish of sea salt. Let rise for 25 minutes and bake at 425° for 15–20 minutes or until lightly browned. Makes 36.

–Sourdough
Gingerbread

Of all the sourdough desserts, this gingerbread is one of the best. Serve with applesauce or whipped cream on top.

1 cup sourdough starter from crock
1⅓ cups whole-wheat flour
1 cup warm water

Combine these ingredients, cover, and let ferment in warm place for at least 12 hours. Add 1 cup of fermented mixture to starter crock. Use the remaining 1½ cups to complete this recipe.

½ cup butter
½ cup brown sugar
1 egg
1 cup molasses
1 teaspoon cinnamon
1 teaspoon ginger
½ teaspoon allspice
Pinch of mace
½ cup whole-wheat flour
½ teaspoon salt
¼ teaspoon soda
1½ cups starter mixture

Cream butter and sugar. Add egg, and beat well. Stir in molasses until well blended. Add spices, flour, salt, and soda, and beat until smooth. Stir in starter. Pour batter into greased square baking pan. Bake at 350° for 55 minutes or until knife inserted in center comes out clean. Serves 9.

SCANDINAVIAN CHRISTMAS SPECIALTIES

Early Scandinavian pioneers and the communities they built in the Pacific Northwest have made a significant culinary impact on the region. These settlers were often first-generation Americans born in Minnesota or the Dakotas, who came west attracted by both the climate and job opportunities as fishermen or loggers.

Communities such as Ballard, once a separate village and now a district of urban Seattle, were established by fishermen of Swedish and Norwegian descent. The small town of Poulsbo, on the other side of the sound, serves as home port for a prosperous fishing fleet. These towns, among others, still proudly display their ethnic heritage through restaurants, shops, and festivals inspired by the "old country" traditions.

Probably no single aspect of Scandinavian cuisine is as popular with the rest of the world as Christmas breads and pastries. There are several Swedish, Norwegian, and Danish bakeries in Seattle alone. These provide hundreds of dozens of special cookies, breads, and pastries for appreciative people throughout Puget Sound. And in many Northwest kitchens, regardless of ethnic origin, specialties such as lefse, krumkake, fattigman, and spritz cookies are a traditional part of Christmas.

Some of these treats require special equipment—a particular pan, a conical wooden roller. Such things can be found in specialty cookware shops. But for those who can't find or don't want to invest in aebleskiver pans and sanbakels tins, here are several traditional recipes that just need ordinary equipment.

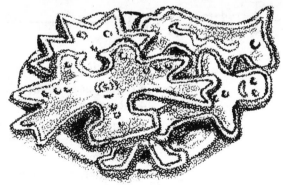

–Christmas Bread––––––––––––––
(Julekake)

2 cups scalded milk
½ cup butter, softened
⅔ cup sugar
2 teaspoons salt
1 teaspoon crushed cardamom seeds
2 packages dry yeast
¼ cup lukewarm water
2 eggs, lightly beaten
8 cups flour
1 cup golden raisins
1 cup chopped citron
1 cup chopped candied cherries

Combine milk, butter, sugar, salt, and cardamom, and cool to lukewarm.
Dissolve yeast in water and pour into milk mixture, stirring well. Add
eggs, stir, and add half the flour, beating until smooth. Let rise in warm
place for 1 hour or until bubbly. Add fruit and remainder of flour. Knead
until smooth. Brush top with melted butter and let rise in warm place until
double in bulk. Divide dough into thirds, place in 3 loaf pans, and let rise
again until double in bulk. Bake at 350° for 1 hour. Makes 3 loaves.

–Fattigman––––––––––––––––

2 eggs
2 egg yolks
4 tablespoons sugar
4 tablesooons heavy cream
1 tablespoon lemon juice
½ teaspoon salt
2 cups flour
Confectioner's sugar

Combine eggs and yolks and beat until light. Add sugar, cream, lemon
juice, salt, and 1 cup flour, and stir until smooth. Add remaining flour and
blend well. Refrigerate dough for at least 2 hours. Roll out on lightly
floured board to ⅛-inch thickness and cut into strips or diamonds. Fry in

deep hot fat (about 375°) for 3 minutes or until golden on both sides. Dust with confectioner's sugar. Makes 24.

–Potato Lefse

There are nearly as many lefse, or potato pancake, recipes as there are good Norwegian cooks. Although special lefse griddles are available, any greased hot griddle will do nicely.

2 cups riced or mashed potatoes
1 tablespoon light cream
1 tablespoon lard
2 teaspoons sugar
½ teaspoon salt
1 cup flour

Cool potatoes and mix with cream and lard. Chill for 1 hour, then add sugar, salt, and flour, and blend thoroughly. Roll mixture into paper-thin rounds, using about ⅓ cup for each. Cook on greased griddle over low heat until lightly browned. Makes 12.

HOLIDAY FAVORITES

Just like everywhere else in America, I am sure, the Christmas holiday season in the Pacific Northwest provides most people with the perfect excuse (or inspiration) for a good party. Whether it is an intimate gathering of close friends or an open house for the entire neighborhood, holiday parties always seem particularly enjoyable. One tradition among several of my favorite households is a holiday brunch, often held late on Christmas morning once the general level of activity has subsided and both parents and children are ready to do some serious eating.

Each kitchen is asked to provide its "best" specialty, usually a baked treat, and the host family puts on the rest. There are often six or eight different cakes, rolls, and buns, in addition to omelets, sausages, bacon, and fruit. And although some of the adults would rather drink Bloody Marys, most have at least one cup of syllabub, a tasty blend of cream, sugar, and sherry said to have originated in pre-Elizabethan England.

–Syllabub

Juice and grated rind of 1 lemon
2 cups heavy cream
½ cup sugar
½ cup sherry

Combine all ingredients and beat until stiff (about 20 minutes with whisk or 5 minutes with electric beater). Refrigerate for 30 minutes and serve. Serves 6.

–Sourdough-Buckwheat–
Pancakes

A magnificent breakfast/brunch is never quite complete without pancakes; and these sourdough-buckwheats are a Northwest standard. Serve with homemade syrup from last summer's raspberries, blueberries, or blackberries.

1 cup sourdough starter
**   from crock**
¾ cup whole-wheat flour
¾ cup buckwheat flour
1 cup warm water

Combine starter, flour, buckwheat, and water. Cover and let ferment overnight. Add 1 cup of fermented mixture to starter crock. Use the remaining 1½ cups to complete this recipe.

1½ cups sourdough-buckwheat mixture
1 teaspoon baking powder
2 tablespoons melted butter
¼ cup instant dry milk
1 teaspoon salt
2 tablespoons honey

Combine sourdough-buckwheat mixture with rest of ingredients and let stand at least 20 minutes. Drop by spoonfuls onto hot oiled griddle. Turn when bubbles break and stay open. Makes 8 4-inch pancakes.

—Hot Cross Buns—————

Although hot cross buns are an Easter tradition, the demand for them at Christmas seems just as great.

1 tablespoon baking yeast
¼ cup warm water
1 cup milk
⅓ cup honey
¼ cup butter
½ teaspoon salt
1 egg
3–4 cups white flour
½ teaspoon cinnamon
1 tablespoon grated orange rind
½ cup currants
½ cup coarsely chopped walnuts
1 egg beaten with 1 tablespoon water
Confectioner's sugar
Lemon juice

Dissolve yeast in water and set aside. Scald milk in small saucepan, add honey and butter, and stir to melt. Then add salt and egg and beat until well blended and cool. Pour into bread bowl, add yeast and half of flour. Beat 100 strokes, then stir in cinnamon, orange rind, currants, and nuts. Add remaining flour a little at a time, blending well. Knead lightly until dough is smooth and let double in bulk in warm place.

Tear off egg-size pieces of dough, shape into round buns, and place in greased long baking pan with edges barely touching. Let rise for 20 minutes and brush tops with beaten egg. Slash a cross in each bun with sharp knife. Bake at 400° for 20 minutes. Remove and cool, dribbling confectioner's sugar moistened with lemon juice over the cross. Makes 3 dozen.

—P.A.Cinnamon Rolls—

There was a restaurant in the country near Seattle that drew crowds from miles away to eat delicious cinnamon rolls, baked in the kitchen every morning. The baker of these goodies is also a friend of mine and obligingly brought a dozen to Christmas brunch last year, much to everyone's pleasure.

—Dough—

1 tablespoon bakers' yeast
¼ cup warm water
¾ cup scalded milk
2 tablespoons honey
3½–4 cups white flour
1 teaspoon salt
3 tablespoons melted butter

—Filling—

¾ cup brown sugar
1½ teaspoons cinnamon
½ cup walnuts, finely chopped
½ cup golden raisins, plumped in boiling water

—Syrup—

4 tablespoons butter
½ cup brown sugar
¼ cup water

Dissolve yeast in water. Cool milk to lukewarm and add to yeast along with honey. Add 1 cup flour to liquid and beat 100 strokes to form "sponge." Let it rest for at least 20 minutes, then add salt and butter. Gradually beat in remaining flour and—when dough becomes too stiff to beat—turn out onto lightly floured board and knead until smooth and satiny. Let rise in a warm place until double in bulk. Punch down and flatten into a rectangle about ¼ inch thick. Sprinkle with brown sugar, cinnamon, nuts, and raisins, and carefully roll up jellyroll-fashion. Cut into 1-inch pieces and place them 1 inch apart in greased long baking pan. Let rise 20 minutes and bake at 375° for 15 minutes.

Boil remaining butter, brown sugar, and water together in small saucepan.

When rolls are lightly brown pour syrup over top and return to oven for 5 minutes more. Serves 4–6.

–Breakfast Scones

These home-baked scones are wonderful and a great excuse for second helpings of the delicious carrot marmalade made from the next recipe.

2 cups white flour
¼ cup wheat germ
3 tablespoons noninstant powdered milk
2½ teaspoons baking powder
1 tablespoon sugar
½ teaspoon salt
⅓ cup butter
⅓ cup currants
2 eggs
⅓ cup milk

Combine flour, wheat germ, milk, baking powder, sugar, and salt until well blended. Cut in butter with two knives until flour mixture resembles corn meal. Add currants. Beat eggs and milk together, make well in flour mixture, and pour in liquid all at once. Combine quickly with fingers and knead a few strokes—just until dough holds together. Divide into 2 pieces, pat them into rounds, and cut each into quarters. Place quarters on ungreased baking sheet and bake at 425° for 15–20 minutes or until golden. Makes 8.

–Carrot Marmalade

5 cups water
1 orange rind, coarsely grated
2 lemon rinds, coarsely grated
4 cups carrots, coarsely grated
Juice of 2 oranges
Juice of 2 lemons
2 cups honey
2 teaspoons cardamom
2 teaspoons powdered ginger
Dash of anise

Pour 3 cups boiling water over orange and lemon rind and let stand over-night. Put into large saucepan with remaining water, carrots, orange and lemon juice, honey, cardamom, ginger, and anise. Bring to a boil and boil hard until very thick, stirring frequently. Pour into sterilized jars and process in boiling water for 10 minutes. Makes 4 pints.

—Aunt Edie's Blintzes—
No Christmas feast would be complete without blintzes.

—Pancakes—

4 eggs
1 cup water
1 cup flour
¼ teaspoon salt
2 teaspoons butter

—Filling—

8 oz. cream cheese, softened
2 cups large-curd cottage cheese
2 tablespoons sugar
1 teaspoon vanilla
½ teaspoon cinnamon (optional)

Mix eggs and water until well blended. Stir together salt and flour. Add liquid to dry ingredients stirring well to remove all lumps. Melt butter in medium frying pan and pour small quantity of batter and swirl pan quickly to form a very thin pancake. Cook over moderate heat on one side only. When pancake is slightly brown but not at all stiff, flip onto plate or counter, cooked side up. Makes 18 5-inch pancakes.

Combine filling ingredients and beat until smooth. Place 2 tablespoons filling along cooked side in center of pancake. Fold edges of pancake tightly over filling and roll up. Bake in long baking pan at 350° with folded side down until golden brown, turning once. Serve with sour cream and fresh blueberries.

CHRISTMAS DINNER

In years when I don't organize a Christmas Day brunch, I usually invite a few close friends and family for dinner late in the afternoon. The long dining table is set with eight or ten places, fir boughs and holly branches grace the center, and lots of candles provide soft festive light. Arriving at four o'clock, everyone is hungry—since all the morning Christmas activity has precluded any serious eating earlier in the day.

Those who feel inspired often contribute part of the feast, but the turkey, rolls, and at least one of the desserts are my job. The festivities begin with a wassail bowl of spiced wine, served hot in small mugs, and plates of smoked salmon, sharp cheese, and melba toast. Everyone, from the oldest to youngest, is bright and happy and ready to share the Christmas spirit. It is a very special day.

The meal begins with an unusual salad, which further stimulates already eager appetites, and then it moves on to the turkey with numerous trimmings. Dessert comes in two or three varieties, and, after, coffee and brandy everyone rolls away from the table—grateful for this extraordinary feast.

–Winter Salad

1 bunch fresh parsley, coarsely shredded
2 cups walnuts, coarsely chopped
4 large pink grapefruit, peeled, sectioned, and coarsely chopped
2 cups pitted black olives, cut into halves
1 cup grated carrots
2 medium onions, thinly sliced
1 cup grated Cheddar cheese
¾ cup olive oil
½ cup cider vinegar
1 small garlic clove, mashed
½ teaspoon Dijon mustard

208

Combine parsley, walnuts, grapefruit, olives, carrots, and onions, and sprinkle with cheese. Combine rest of ingredients until well blended, pour over salad, and toss to mix thoroughly. Serve on bed of lettuce. Serves 8.

–Turkey with Oatmeal Stuffing

20-lb. fresh turkey
1 cup melted bacon fat or vegetable oil
6 medium onions, chopped
1 bunch of celery, coarsely chopped
2 teaspoons fresh sage
2 tablespoons fresh oregano
2 teaspoons fresh thyme
7 cups long-cooking oatmeal
2 cups chopped walnuts
Salt and pepper to taste

In large frying pan sauté onions in fat until wilted, then add celery and stir to coat. Add herbs and oatmeal, stirring to mix thoroughly. Sprinkle on salt and pepper to taste, add walnuts, and stir.

Rinse and pat turkey dry. Fill both front and back cavities with stuffing and sew openings shut. Place in shallow roasting pan and bake at 325° for about 4½ hours, or until thermometer inserted in breast reads 185° and when thickest part of drumstick feels very soft. Serves 15.

–Effie's Famous Sweet Potato Custard

This old family recipe was the delight of my childhood Christmas dinner, especially when topped with marshmallows and pecans and browned under the broiler at the last minute. The marshmallows are gone, but the delight is still there.

**6 large yams, cut into large chunks and
   boiled until tender
2 cups milk
½ cup melted butter
1 cup sugar
6 large eggs
2 teaspoons vanilla**

Peel and mash yams, add milk and butter, and whirl in blender until smooth. In large bowl, combine yam mixture, sugar, eggs, and vanilla, and beat with wooden spoon until thoroughly blended. Pour into long baking pan and bake at 350° for 50 minutes or until center is firm. Serves 8.

–Gingered Tomato Butter

A great condiment and complement to any fowl, especially turkey, tomato butter should be made several months before Christmas—just as the last green tomatoes are ready to come into the kitchen.

**4 large red tomatoes
15 medium green tomatoes
2 lemons, thinly sliced
1 cup water
2 cups sugar
½ teaspoon powdered cloves
2 small pieces ginger
1 tablespoon candied ginger, minced
1 tablespoon candied orange peel, minced**

Blanch, peel, and chop tomatoes, and place in Dutch oven. Add lemon slices and water, and stir well. Add remaining ingredients and cook over low heat, stirring continually, for 30 minutes or until thickened. Pack into clean pint jars and process for 10 minutes in boiling water bath. Makes 6 pints.

–Braised Parsnips

6 tablespoons butter
2 tablespoons brown sugar
3 lbs. parsnips, peeled
  and cut into long thin strips

In medium frying pan, melt butter and stir in sugar. Then sauté parsnips over moderate heat until browned on all sides. Reduce heat, cover, add small amount of water if necessary, and let cook until tender. Serves 8.

–Aunt Mary's Rolls

Plain and simple, these rolls always disappear quickly. A double batch will supply the right number for a big feast like Christmas dinner.

1¼ cups milk
4 tablespoons butter
2 tablespoons honey
1 teaspoon salt
1 tablespoon yeast
¼ cup warm water
4 cups unbleached white flour

Scald milk over medium heat in large saucepan until bubbles form around edge of pan. Melt butter and honey in hot milk, add salt, and stir well. Dissolve yeast in warm water and combine with cooled milk. Beat in 2 cups flour for 100 strokes or until well blended. Add remaining flour until mixture is too stiff to stir. Turn out dough onto floured bread board and knead until smooth and not sticky. Return to bowl and let rise in warm place until double in bulk. Punch down. Pinch off egg-size pieces and form each into smooth ball. Place in greased muffin tins or 1 inch apart on greased baking sheet. Let rise in warm spot for 20 minutes, dot with butter, and bake at 400° for 15 to 20 minutes until golden brown. Makes 36.

–Persimmon Pudding–––

Dessert is the highlight of many Christmas feasts. I usually serve a quite traditional dessert and another one not so readily expected. This persimmon pudding is a pleasant change from the standard plum pudding, and the flan, which follows, is great at any time of year.

1 cup white flour
1 cup sugar
2 teaspoons soda
¼ cup milk
1 teaspoon vanilla
⅓ cup melted butter
1 cup nuts
1 cup raisins
1 cup persimmon pulp
(from 2 large or 3 small persimmons)

Sift flour, sugar, and soda together, and stir in liquids, beating until smooth. Add nuts, raisins, and persimmon pulp, and blend thoroughly. Place in pudding mold, or in pan with tight-fitting lid. Steam for 1½–2 hours or bake at 325° for 1½ hours. Serves 8.

–Easy Flan–––––––––

2 cups milk
2 tablespoons powdered milk
3 eggs
4 tablespoons honey
1 teaspoon vanilla
Dash nutmeg

Beat powdered milk into whole milk, add eggs, and beat until smooth. Add honey, vanilla, and stir until honey dissolves. Pour into soufflé dish and sprinkle lightly with nutmeg. Bake at 325° for 1 hour or until knife inserted into center comes out clean. Serves 6.

INDEX

Abalone, 192
Agaricus mushrooms, 137
   crepes, 137-38
   rosti, 138
Anadama bread, 37-38
Apple(s), 109-12
   -cabbage slaw, 125-26
   cake, 122
   chutney, 124
   cider, 109-10, 112
      brandy cider punch,
        114
      roast pheasant
        baked in, 113
      sparkling, 117-18
   custard, 123-24
   dumplings, 121-22
   for eating, 118
   fritters, 123
   mushroom sauté, 126
   pie, sour cream, 119-21
   stuffed with yams, 125
   wine, 114-17
Apricot
   milkshake, 47
   stuffing, 48
Asparagus, 10-13
   baked, 12-13
   -crab mushroom quiche, 22
   soup, cream of, 11-12
   vinaigrette, 12
Aunt Edie's blintzes, 206
Aunt Mary's rolls, 210

Backpacking in the
   Olympic Mountains, 27-30
Basque potatoes, 94
Beef
   frittata, 21
   jerky, 33
   meatloaf, Edisto Island, 35
Beer waffles, 23
Bercy sauce, 76
Berries, 49
   See also specific types
Biscuit and pancake mix,
   32-33
Blackberry, 55-56
   punch, 56-57
   upside-down cake, 56
Bleu cheese, oysters and, 186
Blintzes, Aunt Edie's, 206
Blueberry
   crackle cake, 58
   muffins, wild, 58
   sour cream pancakes,
      57-58
Boletus mushrooms, 135
   and pear sauce, 136
   -vegetable soup, 135-36
Bouillon, court, 72
Brandied pears, 164
Brandy cider punch, 114

Bread
   Anadama, 37-38
   Aunt Mary's rolls, 210
   Christmas, 200
   cranberry, 89
   hot cross buns, 203
   P.A. cinnamon rolls, 204-5
   really dark rye, 88-89
Breakfast scones, 205
Brownies, good old, 38
Brussels sprouts with cheese
   sauce, 158-59
Buckwheat-sourdough
   pancakes, 202
Butter, gingered tomato, 209

Cabbage
   -apple slaw, 125-26
   curried, 161
   Dutch. 113-14
   Kim chee, 36
   sauerkraut, 161-62
   and Swiss, 160-61
Cake
   blackberry upside-down,
      56
   blueberry crackle, 58
   carrot, 95-96
   pear Kuchen, fresh, 164-65
   rhubarb applesauce, 27
Capers, mayonnaise and, 78
Carrot(s), 94
   cake, 95-96
   compote, 95
   marmalade, 205-6
   and mint, 95
Chanterelles, 130
   curried, 133
   marinated, 134
   pie, 131
   pizza, 132-33
Cheddar cheese
   and chutney omelet,
      French style, 20
   straws, 38
Cheese
   blintzes, Aunt Edie's, 206
   crab baked with almonds
      and, 176-77
   sauce
      baked cod and, 83
      Brussels sprouts with,
        158-59
   strawberry cheese pie, 52
   straws, 38
Cherry(-ies), 44
   chicken and, 48-49
Chicken, 13-15
   and cherries, 48-49
   curry, 30
Chocolate-filbert cream,
   166-67
Chowder

   clam, Island, 61-62
   corn, 100-1
Christmas bread, 200
Christmas dinner, 207
Christmas specialties, 201
   Scandinavian, 199-201
Chutney
   apple, 124
   and cheddar omelet,
      French style, 20
Cider, *see* Apple—cider
Cinnamon rolls, P.A., 204-5
Clam(s), 59-60
   baked, 63
   chowder, Island, 61-62
   geoduck, *see* Geoduck
   razor, 64
   sauce I, 62
   sauce II, 62-63
   steamed, 61
Cod
   and cheese sauce, baked,
      83
   croquettes, 85-86
   seviche, 86
   with vegetables, baked, 84
Compote
   carrot, 95
   fruit, 46
Copper bowl, 16
Corn, 99
   chowder, 100-1
   relish, 100
Court bouillon, 72
Crab (Dungeness), 174-75
   -asparagus mushroom
      quiche, 22
   baked with almonds and
      cheese, 176-77
   Cioppino, 177
   deviled, 175-76
   -stuffed won tons, 178
Cranberry
   bread, 89
   relish, quick, 89
Cream(ed)
   filbert-chocolate, 166-67
   onions, 156
   syllabub, 202
Crepes, mushroom, 137-38
Croquettes, cod, 85-86
Cucumber(s)
   dill chunks, 170
   dill pickles, 168-69
   dill sauce, 78
   dip, 101
   -lime marmalade, 169
Curry(-ied)
   cabbage, 161
   chanterelles, 133
   chicken, 30
   dip, 101
   duck, 151-52

eggs, 35
  sauce, sour cream, 79
  stuffing, for game birds,
    148-49
Custard
  apple, 123-24
  flan, easy, 211
  pie
    pumpkin, 160
    rhubarb, 26
  sweet potato, Effie's
    famous, 208-9

Daiquiris, fresh strawberry, 52
Deer, hunting for elk and,
  141-42
Dill
  cucumber sauce, 78
  sauce, new potatoes in, 93
Dip
  cucumber, 101
  curry, 101
  shrimp, 179
Duck
  curried, 151-52
  roast, 147-48
Duck (geoduck) soup, 67
Dumplings, apple, 121-22
Dungeness, see Crab
Dutch cabbage, 113-14

Effie's famous sweet potato
  custard, 208-9
Eggs, 15
  curried, 35
  See also Custard; Omelets;
    Quiche; Souffle
Elk, hunting for deer and,
  141-42

Fattigman, 200-1
Filberts (hazelnuts), 165
  -chocolate cream, 166-67
  squash soup, 166
Fish
  bottom, 79-80
  rock, 81-82
  seviche, 86
  stew, Puget Sound, 84-85
  wine-baked, 80
  See also specific types
Flan, easy, 211
Fritters
  apple, 123
  mushroom, 140
  oyster, 187
Fruit
  compote, 46
  drinks, fresh, 47
  summertime, 43-44
  See also specific types

Game birds
  curried stuffing for, 148-49
  hunting for, 145-46
  orange sauce for, 149
  preparation of, 146-47
  See also Duck; Pheasant
Geoduck, 64-65
  marinated, 66

steak, 66
Gingerbread, sourdough, 198
Grapes, 107-9
Gravlax, 73-74
Green bean-mushroom
  vinaigrette, 139
Green pepper jelly, 144
Green salsa, 152
Green sauce, 78

Halibut, skewered, 81
Hangtown fry, 187
Hazelnuts, see Filberts
Herbs, 6-7
Hollandaise sauce, 77
Hot cross buns, 203
Huachinago Puget Sound, 82
Hummus, 102

Ice cream, 44
  peach, 45

Jam, raspberry freezer, 55
Jambalaya Alberni, 182
Jelly, pepper, 144
Jerky, beef, 33
Juice, tomato, 167-68
Julekake, 200

Kim chee, 36
Kitsap Peninsula, 170-71

Lasagne, zucchini, 97
Lefse, 201
Lemon parsley sauce, 76
Lentil-zucchini soup, 98-99
Lettuce, 91
  salad, limestone, 92

Mac's Mother's mustard
  sauce, 36
Marmalade, 168
  carrot, 205-6
  cucumber-lime, 169
Marsala peaches, 46
Mayonnaise and capers, 78
Meatloaf, Edisto Island, 35
Milkshake, apricot, 47
Mint, carrots and, 95
Muffins, wild blueberry, 58
Mushroom(s)
  agaricus, 137
    crepes, 137-38
    rösti, 138
  apple sauté, 126
  boletus, 135
    and pear sauce, 136
    -vegetable soup, 135-36
  chanterelle, 130
    curried, 133
    marinated, 134
    pie, 131
    pizza, 132-33
  -crab-asparagus quiche, 22
  hunting, 127-30
  meadow, 139
    fritters, 140
    green bean-mushroom
      vinaigrette, 139
  pine (matsutake), 140

salmon, 140-41
  and spinach frittata, with
    beef, 21
Mussels, 188
  gratinée, 190
  marinière, 189
  sweet-cooked, 189
Mustard sauce, Mac's
  Mother's, 36

Noodles, vegetarian, 31
Nut butter, 33

Oatmeal stuffing, turkey with,
  208
Octopus, 190-91
Olympic Mountains, 173-74
  backpacking in, 27-30
Omelets, 18-19
  cheddar and chutney,
    French style, 20
  frittata, 21
  peach melba, 21
  vegetable, American style,
    20
Onions, creamed, 156
Orange
  roast pheasant, 148
  sauce
    classic, 149
    very, 150
Oysters, 183-84
  and bleu cheese, 186
  and brown sauce, 186
  Cortez, 185
  fritters, 187
  Hangtown fry, 187
  stew, Northwest, 185

P.A. Cinnamon rolls, 204
Pancakes
  blueberry sour cream,
    57-58
  sourdough-buckwheat, 202
Parsley lemon sauce, 76
Parsnips, braised, 210
Peach(es), 44
  in compote, 46
  ice cream, 45
  Marsala, 46
  melba omelet, 21
  tarts, fresh, 45
Pear(s), 162
  brandied, 164
  and cheese, fresh, 163
  ginger, 162-63
  kuchen, fresh, 164-65
  poached stuffed, 163-64
Peas, snow, pork with, 90-91
Pepper jelly, 144
Persimmon pudding, 211
Pheasant
  orange roast, 148
  plum, 153
  roast, baked in apple cider,
    113
  in sour cream sauce,
    150-51
  See also Game birds
Pickles, 168

dill, 168-69
dill chunks, 170
Picnics, 34
Pie
   green tomato, 156-57
   pumpkin custard, 160
   rhubarb custard, 26
   sour cream apple, 119-21
Pike Place market, 42-43
Plum pheasant, 153
Pork
   loin, glazed, 112
   with snow peas, 90-91
Potato(es)
   Basque, 94
   lefse, 201
   new, in dill sauce, 93
Prawns, 178-79
   barbecued, 181
   saute, 180
Pretzels, sourdough, 197-98
Prince mushrooms, see
   Mushrooms—agaricus
Pudding, persimmon, 211
Pumpkin
   custard pie, 160
   soup, 159
Punch, blackberry, 56-57
   brandy cider, 114

Quiche, crab-asparagus
   mushroom, 22

Raspberry(-ies), 54
   freezer jam, 55
   sour cream shortcake, 54
Razor clams, 64
Red snapper, Huachinago
   Puget Sound, 82
Relish
   corn, 100
   cranberry, quick, 89
   zucchini, 171
Rhubarb
   applesauce cake, 27
   custard pie, 26
Rice salad, 36-37
Riddled shrimp, 180-81
Rockfish, 81-82
Rolls
   Aunt Mary's, 210
   P.A. cinnamon, 204-5
Rye bread, really dark, 88-89

Salad
   limestone lettuce, 92
   rice, 36-37
   winter, 297-98
Salmon, 67-72
   baked, 73
   broiling, 70-72
   gravlax (pickled), 73-74
   matsutake, 140-41
   poaching, 72
   preparing and cutting,
     70-71
   sauces for, 76-79
   smoked, 75
     steamed, 73
Salsa
   green, 152
   green tomato, 158
Sauce

Bercy, 76
cheese, baked cod and, 83
clam, 62-63
cucumber dill, 78
dill, new potatoes in, 93
green, 78
green salsa, 152
hollandaise, 77
lemon parsley, 76
mustard, Mac's Mother's,
   36
orange
   classic, 149
   very, 150
pear and boletus, 136
for salmon, 76-79
sour cream curry, 79
veloute, 77
vinaigrette, 79
Sauerkraut, 161-62
Sausage
   glop, 32
   venison, 144
Scallops, 192
Scandinavian Christmas
   specialties, 199-201
Seattle, 42-43
Scones, breakfast, 205
Seafood simmer, 192
Seviche, 86
Shrimp, 178-79
   creole, 183
   dip, 179
   riddled, 180-81
Smelt, 86-87
Snow peas, pork with, 90-91
Souffle, 16
   savory, 16-17
   sweet, 17-18
Souffle dish, 16
Soup
   cream of asparagus, 11-12
   clam chowder, Island,
     61-62
   duck (geoduck), 67
   lentil-zucchini, 98-99
   pumpkin, 159
   strawberry, 53
   zucchini, 99
Sour cream
   apple pie, 119-21
   blueberry pancakes, 57-58
   curry sauce, 79
   raspberry shortcake, 54
   sauce, pheasant in, 150-51
Sourdough, 195-96
   bread, 195-96
   basic, 196
   French, 197
   gingerbread, 198
   pretzels, 197-98
Spanish ala, 31
Spinach
   baked, 92-93
   and mushroom frittata,
     with beef, 21
Squid, 190

savory, 190-91
Steelhead trout, see Trout,
   steelhead
Stew
   oyster, northwest, 185
   vegetable, 103
Stir-fried vegetables, 104-5
Stir-frying, 104
Strawberry(-ies), 49-51
   cheese pie, 52
   daiquiris, fresh, 52
   soup, 53
Stuffing
   apricot, 48
   curried, 148-49
   oatmeal, turkey with, 208
Sweet potato custard, Effie's
   Famous, 208-9
Syllabub, 201-2

Tarts, fresh peach, 45
Tempura, vegetable, 105
Tomato
   butter, gingered, 209
   green
     chutney, 157
     pie, 156
     salsa, 158
   juice, 167-68
   salad, marinated, 37
Trout, steelhead, 192-93
   baked, 194
   Irish Fish Company
   pan-fried, 193-94
Turkey with oatmeal stuffing,
   208

Vegetable(s)
   baked greens, 92-93
   blanching, 167
   cod with, baked, 84
   garden, 90
     late, 154
     planting, 25-26
   marinade, 102
   omelet, American style, 20
   stew, 103
   stir-fried, 104-5
   tempura, 105
Vegetarian noodles, 31
Veloute sauce, 77
Venison, 143
   chops, 143
   roast, 143-44
   sausage, 144

Waffles, beer, 23
Wine, 107-9
   apple, 114-17
   -baked fish, 80
   marsala (or other sweet
     wine), peaches in, 46
Won tons, crab-stuffed, 178

Yams, apples stuffed with,
   125

Zucchini, 96
   lasagne, 97
   -lentil soup, 98-99
   patties, 98
   relish, 171
   soup, 99